THE *flip·flop* CEO

ISBN: 978-0-615-42449-1

Cover designed by: SeaSaw Marketing

Interior designed by: Claire Fontana

Visit us on the web:

www.theflipflopceo.com

From Lory and Janine:

Since embracing this business, our lives have been filled with so many inspirational, powerful and compassionate friends. Because of all of you, we've gotten a glimpse of what is possible in this world. We're forever grateful to be a part of such a life-changing community. We are truly better together.

Whitney, you are exactly what we were searching for! You immediately caught the vision, immersed yourself in the experience, and became a passionate advocate of this profession. Thank you for putting your *whole* self into this project to authentically communicate our voice. We admire your sass, wisdom and dedication. Thank you for making our dream a reality.

Dane, you are a part of who we are and everything we do. We adore you. Without you, Melissa Linden and Debbie Onsager, this book might not have been written. Each of you have been our angels along the way. Thank you for being our sounding board, with your unwavering commitment to support us in speaking our truth. Words cannot adequately convey our appreciation for your unconditional love, guidance and honesty. We cherish your friendship.

To our Shower Curtain Girls, Dana Eriksson, Jen Furrier, Andrea Scholer, Debi Tombazian and Kerri Laryea, thank you for insisting that there was a book within us and a story that had to be told.

To Bevla, thank you for *knowing* that Whitney was the one.

To Jodi Low and Renee Dee, for inspiring our dream. Thank you, girlfriends!!

For sharing your incredible love and light, thank you, Dr. Tanda Cook, Dr. Sarah Marshall, Jesse Neidt, Roxanne Melker, Melissa Haupt and Chrissa Michelle.

We are also so grateful to all of our friends, including everyone mentioned above, who took the time to read our book and provide invaluable feedback... Hope Baker, Stasia Trivison, Valerie Edwards, Iain Pritchard, Jill Ellis, Audra Berger, Diane Ryan, Jill Lohmiller, Tom and Lorraine Callaghan, Catherine Swinscoe, Doreen Bishop, Billie Young, Melissa Krieger, Kendra Katter, Crystal Barcello, Donna Price, Ericka Hirons, Jessica Emes, Chantelle Braham, Jamie Wieferich, Cathy Swann, Carrie Severson, Bobcat Brown, Melinda Adams-Johnson, Shari Weller, Kim Mylls, Jodi Towns, Geri Amster, Barbeth Pinkney, Meg McPhinney,

Todd Hill, Rosemary Price, and Gayle Kelly. We appreciate you more than our words could possibly express!

We also want to thank each one of you, who shared your story with us, for our book. What an inspiring group of leaders you are. Thank you all for exemplifying what is possible when belief and commitment collide!

Doug and Marcus, you are the wind beneath our wings. Marcus, you are the best dad in the whole world. Thank you for every second that you spent taking such good care of Parker and Hudson when Mommy and TaTa couldn't be there. Doug, thank you for your wisdom and tireless support. We appreciate all of the sacrifices you've made so that our book could be written. We love the "big" and "little" men in our lives with all of our hearts!

From Whitney:

Lory and Janine, thank you for sharing your vision, your hearts and your lives with me. It is such an honor to be a part of this project. Lory, you blazed a trail that a lot of us walk on today. Thanks for having the courage to stick with it.

To Laura Russell, Jamie Rubin, Anjuli Fiedler and Pamela Spycher, thank you for being such great friends, and for taking the time to review the book. Your feedback is priceless.

Bevla, thank you for being the bright, beautiful magnet that brought us all together. You are one of a kind.

I am very blessed to have a group of comrades and loved ones who not only support me in my zany endeavors, they join me in them. They are my mastermind group, book editors, vacation buddies, business partners and best friends. To Ramona, Samara, Kate, Christina, Blythe and Rob, thank you for sharing this journey with me. I freakin' love you guys.

The trajectory of my life changed for the better when I stumbled upon this project, and the business model of network marketing. I have the heavens to thank for that.

To all of our book readers, thank you for putting up with this little yearbook signing. If you're shocked or offended by anything in the book, I take full responsibility for it.

When you change the way you look at things,
the things you look at change.

Wayne Dyer

A Flip-Flop CEO:

Doesn't do alarm clocks, bosses, or cubicles.

Makes up her own mind.

Thinks in terms of possibilities, not probabilities.

Lives her life by design.

Doesn't do hourly *or* salary; she earns *residual* income.

Makes money *and* a difference... in her flip-flops.

Table of Contents

Introduction

We are mother and daughter. So naturally, we don't always agree.

In fact, the biggest bone of contention in our relationship to date is what inspired this book—the subject of network marketing. It came into our lives eight years ago, when one of us decided to pursue it with gusto and the other resisted it with might. We battled for over a year.

Eventually, after lengthy periods of arguments, tears and silence, we landed in a place where we finally saw eye to eye. Today, we've both built thriving network marketing businesses and have fulfilled *many* of our lifelong dreams, the biggest of which is working *together*.

We wrote this book because, while the divide in *our* perspectives of this industry is now bridged, it still exists in other families, friendships and society at large. On one side are the insiders—people who believe in the business model, hopeful of the possibilities it presents, frustrated that others don't see it. On the other are the outsiders, skeptical of all the promises, annoyed and offended that it keeps showing up. In the middle are the people who have *no idea what it is.*

Wherever you stand, this book is for you. And there are a couple of things we hope you get out of reading it. The first is a brand new outlook on the network marketing industry. The second, and most important, is a heartfelt realization that you can have more, and *deserve more*, in your life than others claim is possible.

Our message may seem tough in parts, but we promise it truly comes from a place of love. So if we sound a little feisty, it's because we're fired up about this topic. We know that when most people hear the words "network marketing," they instantly plug their ears, and we didn't want to get tuned out.

When we decided that this book needed to be written, we went in search of someone who could help communicate our voice. We found the perfect fit, in the form of an entrepreneur, writer and recovering attorney, who ironically despised network marketing. But there are no accidents.

Today, she is not only a believer, but a successful network marketer and our co-author as well.

We don't claim to be experts on the subject of network marketing. We're just living proof that it *does* work, and you *can* have it all. This industry has given us the gift of a lifetime—the ability to plan our work around our life rather than our life around our work. And now we want to share that gift, in the form of this book, with you.

Our complete stories can be found in the Afterword. Inspirational stories from other Flip-Flop CEOs can be found in the middle of the book.

Chapter One

Get a Life

> The truth will set you free, but first it will make you mad.
>
> *M. Scott Peck*

We don't mean to be rude, but your life could use a face-lift.

Correct us if we're wrong, but you'd rather get a colonoscopy than go to work tomorrow. The last time you felt well-rested was in college. Your salary doesn't budge. Your bonuses are abysmal. Your retirement fund has gone from being a nest egg to a goose egg, and your couch has more money than your savings account.

Sound familiar?

Day in and day out, you fume in rush hour traffic while you cuddle your espresso instead of your kids. You drag your laptop on vacation and your phone to the gym. You're a prisoner to your list of things to do. You have money, but no time. Or time, but no money. And you are tragically un-fun.

But that's not the worst part.

The worst part is that unless you make a move, nothing will change. Tomorrow will be the same as today. Next week will be the same as tomorrow. Unless, of course, there's a big giant recession looming—then it will get worse.

Don't shoot the messengers. We just want to help. We want you to know that you have options.

We're not talking about a second job. We're not talking about winning the lottery. We're not talking about "doing what you love and expecting the money to follow." (That only worked for Oprah.)

We're talking about something you've probably heard of before, something you might have dismissed until now, something lurking… right under your nose. We're talking about network marketing.

Yes, we said it—*network marketing.*

Now, we're not stupid. We know that network marketing still gets a bad rap, and that you'd rather take on a paper route than be caught doing it. We know you have a fancy title and an image to uphold, and that you're getting used to that company car. We get that you have a business to run, with your name on the door. And we see from your license plate that you've earned a degree.

Don't worry, we felt the same way not that long ago. In fact, prior to doing our research on network marketing, we were some of the biggest haters and skeptics around. Let's face it, the industry does have a checkered past, and some network marketers still make the whole place look like a carnival. But that's not a good enough reason to be deterred. That's not a reason to dismiss what could be a viable and credible financial opportunity for *you*.

Trust us, we've done it all. We've been corporate rat-racers, passionate entrepreneurs and loyal employees. We've had careers we loved with salaries we hated, and careers we hated with salaries we loved. So believe us when we say that network marketing is one of the greatest ways to earn a buck.

We wrote this book not to convince you, but to inform you—to flip your frame of reference about an industry that is gravely misunderstood. We wrote this book because we want you to get a life, and a *good* one at that.

Chapter Two

Get a Clue

> I'd rather have 1% of 100 people's efforts than 100% of my own.
>
> *John Paul Getty*

Most people have some idea of what network marketing is. At least, they think they do. In reality their knowledge is about as up-to-date as a perm, but we'll get to that later.

Network marketing, also known as multi-level marketing, is a system for marketing and distributing products. It's essentially word-of-mouth advertising.

Companies that use network marketing systems are really no different from other companies, except for how they make their products known. Instead of investing in billboards, fancy magazine spreads, celebrity endorsements and giant ad agencies, they spend most of their dollars on people.

Yep, that's right—they pay *people* to spread the word. And rather than invest in pricey distributors, middlemen and retail space to get the goods from A to B (say, a can of soda from plant to consumer), they again use people, or nowadays, allow purchases to be made online.

Before the Internet was invented, network marketing was a different animal altogether. Because there was no such thing as e-commerce, people in network marketing companies acted as virtual storefronts, either going from door-to-door or person-to-person to move a product. It was time-consuming and, often times, annoying. Network marketers also had to purchase the products ahead of time, which meant they were left with the burdens of inventory and delivery.

Today, consumers are cyber-savvy, and enjoy buying things online. So with network marketing, they hear about a product from a person who actually uses it, maybe check out a sample, and a mouse-click later, they're done. The products go directly from company to doorstep. Services are the same as goods—someone learns about it, goes online, signs up for the service and *poof!*, it's delivered. All the network marketers do is make the recommendation and connection.

Many experts believe that network marketing is one of the fastest and most efficient ways for a company to move a product. If you think about it, that makes sense. How fast does your online social network grow? How soon after a rumor gets started does the entire office know the scoop? Well, that's how fast a company can reach the masses with network marketing.

With that kind of market penetration, it's no wonder that the industry does $114 billion in global sales a year. Even some of the world's most well-known corporations, including Jockey, Citigroup, Sprint, Verizon, and most successful entrepreneurs, including Donald Trump and Warren Buffet, are venturing into the network marketing world.

Let's face it: newspapers are becoming obsolete; commercials are getting lost in fast forward; pop-up ads are being ignored. What that means is that companies are desperate for innovative ways to reach their buyers. Turns out, the age-old practice of telling a friend still reigns supreme.

Businesses aren't the only ones who like network marketing. Consumers like it, too. That's because on average, the products are a better deal than their retail counterparts. Since the companies are saving so much money by slashing marketing and distribution budgets, they can afford to create high-quality products, pay their network marketers fantastic salaries and still save their end users a pretty penny.

And who doesn't love a good bargain?

How Network Marketers Get Paid

The only people who love network marketing more than the companies and customers are the network marketers themselves. Also known as independent distributors, consultants, or representatives, these are the people who get paid to spread the word. And *how* they get paid is pretty cool.

Although it varies among companies, in general, a network marketer—let's call her Jane—gets a commission on all the goods bought by people she referred to the company. That's the *first part*. These people aren't in the business of network marketing—they're just customers of the company who were referred by Jane. And in some cases, Jane wouldn't even complete the transaction herself. Instead, she would introduce her friends to the products and refer them to the website, where they can shop by themselves.

In that respect, it's a lot like direct selling (of encyclopedia and vacuum fame), but revolutionized by the World Wide Web.

So let's review. For now, Jane gets paid to talk about products she loves. Nice.

But that's not the best part. The *best part* about network marketing is that Jane also gets paid a commission on purchases made by people she hasn't personally talked to at all.

Let us explain.

Like we said, in network marketing, consultants are compensated on the purchases made by their own referrals. But they can also earn commissions on the purchases made by their *network's* referrals as well. That means if Jane connects four people to the business, and they each do the same, Jane will have 21 people in her network, including herself. And she will get paid on each and every referral those 21 people make, *in addition to her own*. In most network marketing companies, she can even get paid on her network's personal purchases, too.

Here's an illustration:

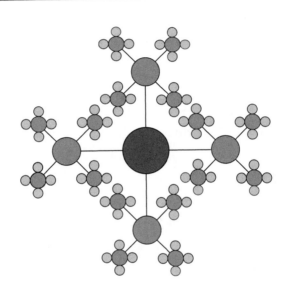

This is an example of a typical network of representatives. When Jane joins the business, she will be at the center of her network. Anyone who later joins her team will be in her network, *and* at the center of their own network.

As you can see, this math can go on and on. Anyone can continue the referral process (three more, five more, ten more), and as a result, Jane's network of independent reps and happy shoppers will expand. Over time, she can actually get paid on the purchases of hundreds or even thousands of people.

And that's the power of a network. That, my friends, is *leverage*.

If real estate is about location, location, location, then network marketing is about *leverage, leverage, leverage*. Leverage is about investing in something once, and getting paid for it again and again. Investors have leverage—their money grows money on its own. The founder of a restaurant franchise has leverage—she built a template for one business, but gets paid on ten more. An entrepreneur who automates a system has leverage—an hour's worth of work saved him fifty. And network marketers have *leverage*—they can have five conversations about a product, and get paid for five thousand. They can train a tiny team of people, and end up with an army.

We know what you're thinking—this sounds like a pyramid scheme. No, we're not psychic; we've just been around this block before. Don't worry, we'll cover that soon.

For now, let's get to the good stuff—what's so great about network marketing.

> The difference between the wealthy and everyone else is leverage. Either you've got it, or your boss does.
>
> Tim Sales, Network Marketing Expert, Author, and Trainer

Get the Facts

- The Direct Selling Association, which also represents network marketing companies, recently celebrated its 100th anniversary. [i]

- As of 2010, 16.1 million people are registered network marketers in the United States. [ii]

- As of 2008, 65 million people are registered network marketers worldwide. [iii]

- United States online retail sales, which rose 12.6% to $176.2 billion in 2010, are expected to grow at a compound annual rate of 10% through the year 2015. [iv]

- In 2010, between "Black Friday" and "Cyber Monday" (the Friday, Saturday and Sunday after Thanksgiving), 33.6% of all shoppers made their purchases online, up 10% from the year before. [v]

Chapter Three

Get This

> There are those who live in a dream
> world, and there are some who face reality;
> and then there are those who
> turn one into the other.
>
> *Douglas H. Everett*

Now, obviously we think network marketing is an ingenious concept; otherwise we wouldn't be doing it. But the question isn't whether network marketing is the right or wrong profession. The question is whether it's right for *you*.

So we'll just tell you what *we* love about it, and you can decide for yourself.

The Top Reasons We Dig This Gig

#1: You Don't Have to Trade Time for Money

Whether you're an employee, freelancer or small business owner, whether you make $10 an hour or $10,000, the trap is the same. You want the paycheck? You do the time.

Face it, that's how most of us were raised—to believe that we had to *earn* our living with an "honest day's work." But *let's be honest*, that system is broken. It's an exhausting way to live, and it's not getting easier anytime soon.

Network marketing is entirely different. It's not about trading time for money, or hours in and dollars out. It's about *residual income*—income that compounds upon itself—that pays time and time again for an initial phase of work.

Everyone in the world wants residual income. People write books for it, launch companies for it, invent products for it, film movies for it—all in the name of making money while they sleep. But those paths are incredibly difficult, and even riskier to boot. Network marketing is one of the only places where residual income is a realistic possibility for the *rest of us*.

In network marketing, residual income grows from three basic steps: (1) learning about the company's offering; (2) spreading the word about it; and (3) teaching other people to do the same. Do this a few times, and before you know it, you're cloned. The people you trained train their own, who in turn do the same. It's a ripple effect, that all started by you throwing a stone.

Now *that's* a good trade.

Whether you're feeling sick, or just plain sick of work, you probably don't have a good exit plan—not for tomorrow *or* when you're 65. Well, at least not if you want to live comfortably. But in network marketing, a successful business can run itself without you. Sure, it takes time to get to that point—they don't sprout up overnight—but it's nice to know that eventually you can take a time out (or ten), and the paycheck will never know.

> On the front end [of network marketing], you work very hard and expect nothing in return. On the back end you're paid far more than you worked for.
>
> Dr. Tom Barrett, Author and Network Marketing Expert

In the beginning, I was just a product user. It took me a few years to really get into the business of network marketing. I was raising kids. I wasn't working like a pitbull for 20 hours a week. If someone does that, they can likely replace a corporate income within a year. It all depends on the time and other issues they have going on in their life. Fortunately, there are many ways to build a network marketing business.

Valerie Aloisio, Network Marketer

#2: Freedom and Flexibility

Work in your pajamas, *check*. Long lunches with friends, *check*. Run errands mid-day, lose the commute, stay at home with your kids when they're sick—*check, check, check*.

A successful network marketing business allows you to plan your work around your life, instead of your life around your work. Open the calendar, block out the most important things to do, and work *around* them. Your office can be the local coffee shop, a nice resort, a friend's house or your couch. It's up to you.

Even better, you don't just get to decide where you want to work; you can decide where you want to *live*. Do you want to be closer to family and friends? Are you tired of the horrible weather where you are? Welcome to the world of choices! Thanks to technology, you can plug into your business from any corner of the globe.

On top of that, network marketing offers you the flexibility to grow your business at your own pace. You can literally fit it into the cracks and crevices of life—a happy hour here, a coffee chat there, a phone call on your way to work. Before you know it, that tiny infant that required so much attention will be a full grown adult on its own.

> I did network marketing while I was pregnant, had two kids, and was working full-time. I replaced my Corporate America income and reached the top level of the company in less than 6 months. It was a lot of work to do it so quickly, but it's do-able.
>
> Lisa DeMayo, Network Marketer

#3: A Business in a Box

These days, people want the benefits of owning a business (tax write-offs, anyone?) but without the headache.

Network marketing offers just that—no product development, research, manufacturing, hiring, firing, designing, negotiating, managing, shipping, receiving, planning or billing. No lawyers, accountants, patents, logos, storefronts or office space. You don't even have to come up with a great idea! Network marketers have the best of both worlds—an infrastructure and proven product or service to plug right into, but without the same risk or expense.

But that's not all. The best part is that network marketing companies have some of the most helpful and comprehensive training around. From product demonstrations and seminars, to national conferences and courses on personal growth, you can attend, join, log on or replay, anytime you need information and support. In that respect, it's like a business school, but where the tuition is practically free.

Yeah, we know there's nothing fancy about a business in a box, but sitting on the beach instead of in a cubicle is pretty glamorous, don't you think?

#4: You Get Paid What You're Worth

No time cards, hourly commitments, or staring at the clock. In network marketing, the compensation is simple— you get paid for your *effectiveness*, not your effort. The better you are at what you do, the more you get paid. And the less time you have to spend doing it.

Now, this isn't the part where we tell you that you can become a rock star overnight. This isn't where we promise you millions. But this is where we tell you that the income potential in network marketing is far greater than in most other industries.

It's true. Network marketing isn't about door-to-door sales anymore. It isn't about $20 here and $40 there. The real business of network marketing is about getting a paycheck from the company for your work, and a good one at that.

Unlike any other job or career, in this business, people who have the exact same title or started at the exact same time can make *vastly* different amounts of money. There are people who have been in it for years, making less than $25 a month, and people who have been in it for months, replacing six-figure incomes. Some of the highest earners in network marketing have been known to make hundreds of thousands of dollars per month (yes, you read that right—*per month*), and a significant amount of that income is passive.

Truthfully, the statistics suggest that this won't be most of us. It's estimated that less than 3% of the people in network marketing make that kind of "gangster" money. But a large number of people still make a great living (that either substantially supplements, matches or exceeds their regular income). So if that sounds good to you, it's important to understand how it all works.

We know what you're thinking: how is it possible that companies can afford to pay such high salaries? Where the heck is that money coming from? *It sounds too good to be true.*

Well, it isn't. And the answer is simple. It comes from cutting out the middlemen—the layers and layers of people and entities that get paid for marketing and distribution. These can typically represent millions of dollars in costs that don't add *any* value to the products themselves.

We realize that sounds abstract to a lot of people, especially if they've never been behind the scenes of a business. So to fully illustrate just how much extra dough network marketing companies are saving by doing this, and how they can issue such large paychecks without breaking the bank, let's look at an example.

Take soda pop for instance: after they're done concocting the recipe, designing the packaging and manufacturing it, the average beverage company has spent maybe three to ten cents a can—*max*—and even less per ounce if it's headed for fountains.

Now they have to get that soda into your hands, the drinker. They do that through grocery stores, mini-marts, movie theaters, restaurants, vending machines, ballparks and more. But forming relationships with these places is no easy task. They have to get their attention, just like they have to get yours. They do *that* through brokers, agents, distributors and sales reps.

That's not all. Just because the soda is on the shelf doesn't mean you'll buy it. They still have to convince *you* to choose their brand over the hundreds of others in contention. They do *that* through marketing—agencies, billboards, commercials, direct mail, coupons, magazine spreads, sponsorships, web ads and spokespeople. As if that weren't enough, they also pay highly-trained publicists to finagle a little "free" press, too.

So let's review—these are all the folks who might have gotten paid for your soda:

- Manufacturer/Factory
- Distributor
- Wholesaler
- Agent
- Broker
- Sales representative
- Ad agency
- Publicist
- Spokesperson
- Media outlets (TV network, magazine, website, billboard owner)

And who paid them? *You* did—fifty cents at the grocery store, a dollar at the vending machine, a buck-fifty at the fast food joint, three dollars at the theater and five dollars at the ballpark or concert. Your final price depends on the individual expenses of these entities, the biggest of which is real estate. Yep, that's right—you paid to turn their lights on, too.

Here's a chart to show you the breakdown.

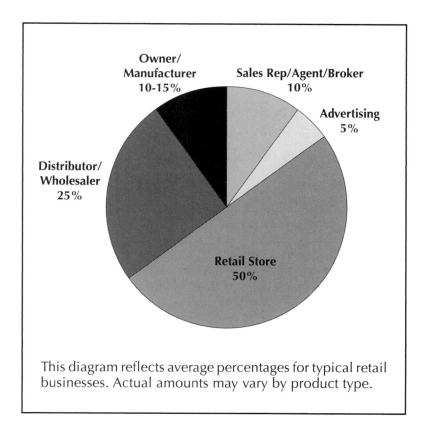

This diagram reflects average percentages for typical retail businesses. Actual amounts may vary by product type.

Feel suckered? You should. The bulk of what you're paying isn't for the product at all. *You're paying to hear about it.*

Now, do you feel inspired to cut some costs for yourself and your friends? Is word-of-mouth marketing starting to make some sense? Good. Let's take a look at the network marketing distribution model on the next page.

See the difference? All that money the company is saving gets passed on to other people—to you, the consumer (so you can get high quality products for a *cheaper* price), and to the network marketer, the person who's actually using it, as opposed to some supermodel on TV.

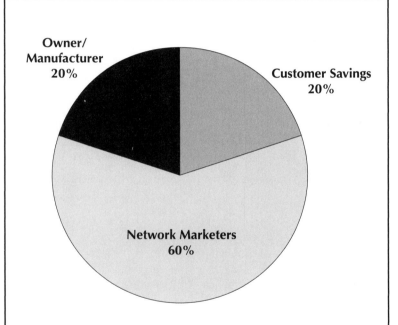

This diagram reflects average percentages for typical network marketing businesses. Actual amounts may vary by product type.

Here it is again!

So the next time you hear about some huge network marketing success story and think the whole thing is just hogwash, consider this—it *might* be hype (we can't prevent creeps from misrepresenting incomes), but it might also be *very true*.

> Corporations like network marketing because they're paying for advertising that benefits the consumer. If a company like T-Mobile hires Catherine Zeta Jones, and pays her $20 million, that $20 million doesn't benefit the consumer, as charming as she is. In network marketing, the same $20 million goes to distributors who have (hopefully) mastered the product and are able to explain it to the consumer.
>
> Tim Sales, Network Marketing Expert, Author, and Trainer

We could go on and on about what network marketing money has done to transform people's lives, from eliminating debt to funding businesses, hobbies, medical needs, vacations, college educations, cars, homes and more. It's given people the freedom to play, retire, work less, donate more and *enjoy* their family and friends. Whatever the case, *you* get to decide. It's *your* need. It's *your* dream. So it's *your* choice.

We realize that these days, people aren't that great at dreaming. Somewhere along the way, all the visions and fairy tales they had as children got squashed by the real world. Well, it's time to get them back. It's time to flex that imagination muscle and kick it into gear.

So you tell us. What's on your wish list? What could you do with more time and more money?

It seems like everyone has a different answer to this question. For some, it's just a matter of finally getting that pair of designer jeans they've been coveting; for others, it's a closet full of custom haute couture. Some folks just want a brand new piece of furniture, or to fix those nagging repairs around the house. Others are aiming for the entire remodel, or even a second home. Maybe you'd like a little extra cash to be able to eat out whenever you want? Or enough to hire your own personal chef.

Wouldn't it be nice to have the money to visit friends and loved ones who live far away? Care to fly there First Class? Would you like to spoil your kids on Christmas? Or yourself, your parents, and your friends... *all year long?* What about adopting a family in need for the holidays? Or five? Or even ten? How about donating your money *and* your time to your favorite cause, mission or cure?

Maybe it's just the ability to pay your bills on time, or spend money on yourself without the guilt. Like we said, it's up to you. You can be practical, you can be lavish. You can save yourself, or you can save the world.

Whatever you decide, just remember—network marketing itself doesn't have to be your dream. It doesn't even have to be your passion. But maybe, *just maybe*, it can pay for what is.

> The potential in this industry is far greater than people realize. But the masses have a hard time wrapping their brain around the numbers. I've had months where I've made more in one month than high level executives do in a year. But if you talk about network marketing to people who are making 30, 50 or 90 grand a year, they don't believe this. They dismiss you right out of the gate. It's a mind-set, and they don't have it yet.
>
> Jeff Van Blaricum, Network Marketer

#5: You Get to Choose Who You Work With

We're not gonna lie, one of the reasons we like network marketing is because it's like summer camp, for adults. You get to meet amazing new people, work with the friends and loved ones you choose, train with the best mentors around, and hang with successful, positive folks whose primary goal is to help YOU. Yes, it's as fun as it sounds.

In network marketing, the camaraderie is built in. You simply can't get rich by yourself. Think about it. The only way for you to reach your goals is by helping other people reach theirs. So you're in business *for* yourself, but never *by* yourself. What's not to love?

Say goodbye to those annoying co-workers, the back-stabbing, tattling and cut-throat environments. This is a brand new kind of tribe.

#6: You Don't Need a Huge Network to be Successful

Perhaps the biggest misconception about network marketing is that you have to have a huge network and hundreds of friends to be successful. That couldn't be further from the truth. In fact, you don't even have to have *ten* friends to be successful. If network marketing were door-to-door sales, the number of clients would matter. But in network marketing, your net*work* is your net *worth*— cheesy, but true. And remember, your "network" will most likely consist of people you didn't originally know.

Allow us to illustrate the beauty of this concept by using an example of something you already do. Let's take your favorite restaurant. You love it, right? So you tell two friends about how much you love it. They each decide to try it, and they love it too. So they tell their friends, who in turn do the same. If this continues, within a few weeks a few dozen people will be eating at the same restaurant (and talking about it, tweeting about it, blogging about it)... all because of *you*.

Now let's assume that you told two more people about that same restaurant, for a total of four, and they each told four, with a similar progression. Now, in the same amount of time, hundreds or even thousands of people—most of whom you've never met—are eating at the same restaurant (and talking about it, tweeting about it, blogging about it)... all because of *you*. Remember, the difference in the beginning was only two people. The difference in the end was *thousands*. That's the power of multiplication.

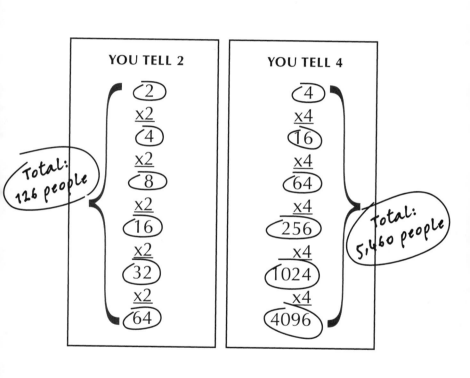

> You can change your whole future… slowly, steadily, and deliberately… by doing something that you've been doing all of your life without realizing it—making referrals.
>
> Nancy Failla, Network Marketing Author and Trainer

You didn't have to quit your job to do this, or talk to hundreds of people. Neither did your friends. This is just how word of mouth works. With a few initial connections, you can have *exponential* results.

Obviously, these diagrams reflect exact duplication. The real world of network marketing doesn't look this perfect (it varies as much as the people who do it). Yet the potential is there. And in some cases, it's even greater than this. The numbers are entirely up to you and your team.

As you can see, this isn't a get-rich-quick scheme (although in most cases it's a get-rich-quicker-than-getting-a-Ph.D-scheme). This is a legitimate business opportunity that takes time and energy to build. *We can't emphasize that enough.* But once the foundation is laid, it's a business that will pay dividends in perpetuity.

Now pay attention. As you can clearly see, you didn't have to be a great salesperson to have success with this system. You weren't a sales rep for the restaurant; you were just a customer who became a loyal fan.

Network marketing is no different. It's about selecting a company you can authentically promote, finding a handful of customers to share it with (you can even be your own customer) and building an organization of people who do the same, one small layer at a time. To do that, you don't need good *salesmanship*; you need good systems, strategy and leadership.

The best network marketers are people who learn to teach, help, mentor and empower other people. Not a *ton* of other people; just *some* other people. Okay?

So, if your network is small or you're not a salesperson, come on in. If you're bad at helping people, *adiós*.

> Having two people in your circle who understand network marketing is way better than having two-hundred who don't. All of the compensation plans are different, but in general with network marketing, if you have three to four solid business builders, you can have a huge team within three to five years.
>
> Leanne Grechulk, Network Marketer

#7: Turn an Expense into Income

Yes, you read that right—turn something that *costs* you money into something that *makes* you money. We know, we know—how is that possible? Well, when you redirect your spending to your own company, you're getting paid to give yourself business. Makes sense, right? If you owned Coke, would you buy a Pepsi? Probably not.

Also, like we said, network marketing products are generally lower in cost (for the same or better quality) than their retail counterparts, which can result in even bigger savings. And some companies offer their independent consultants the perk of added discounts on top of that.

Even better, you get all the tax benefits of owning and operating a home-based business. For some people, especially those in traditional employment, the tax breaks can be a huge and welcome relief.

So whether you want to save money or make money, the choice is yours. Network marketing lets you play both sides of your coins.

#8: Make a Difference with Your Dollars

You hear it all the time—shop local, support your Mom and Pop store, be loyal to the little guy.

It's all the same thing—keep the money close to home. Help your family, your friends, your neighbor, your community. Do it with the purchases you already plan to make.

We're not saying that network marketing companies are the equivalent of the corner store; they're clearly far larger than that. What we're saying is that they work with a lot of independent representatives who are. These are people who are no different from any other small business owner in your town. Their taxes and profit will be put back into your school systems, parks, businesses, housing market and municipal programs. They're some of the best investments you can make.

Whether it's the single mom next door, the friend who got downsized or the struggling family trying to save their home, network marketing is someone's livelihood—someone connected to *you*.

So, the next time you consider buying a bar of soap, a vitamin or specialty item from a giant chain, please, consider the source.

#9: Take Charge of Your Financial Future

For many of us, the fate of our future is in someone else's hands. Day in and out, many of us sit around waiting for the other shoe to drop—to be told that we're no longer of use.

Network marketing allows you take back the control. You decide *how* to grow your business, how *big* to grow your business, *where* to grow your business, and *when*. You're not confined to someone else's list, location, rules or constraints. The only limits are the ones you set.

In this day and age, it can be frightening to feel like your financial bottom line is a matter of fate. With network marketing, whether you do it alongside your job or instead of it, it's just nice to know that when your family needs more bacon, you can bring it home.

#10: The Network Marketing Industry is Poised to Explode

Network marketing is here to stay. But that doesn't mean it will stay the same. On the contrary, all signs suggest that network marketing is about to embark on one of its largest growth spurts yet, and that means higher numbers in everyone's bottom line.

The Economic Outlook

Like we said, in this frightening economic climate, people are looking for a back-up plan—a way to supplement (or even replace) their income with something that doesn't eclipse their full-time work. The problem is that many of the options are horrendous. Getting a second job requires a lot more time. Starting a traditional business requires a lot more time *and money*. Network marketing, on the other hand, requires only a little of both.

Whether it's an extra $300 to chip away at some debt, $2000 to really get ahead, or the goal of turning a Plan B into a Plan A, in network marketing the choice is yours. The amount you make is directly proportional to what you put in. Now *that's* security.

Because of this, people from all walks of life will continue to explore network marketing on their lunch hours and weekends. As a result, network marketers will be in the right place at the right time.

The Rise of Professionalism in Network Marketing

Network marketing certainly has a reputation for welcoming the otherwise unemployable people of the world. And so long as sign-up fees are low, and the income potential remains as great as it is, that won't change.

What *will* change over time is the increase in professional and formally-educated people joining network marketing companies.

Even before white collar workers were getting laid off by the thousands, they were turning to network marketing. There are a few reasons for that. First, the idea of getting paid what you're worth, as opposed to some set salary, is incredibly alluring for talented people. Many of these executives had great jobs, but were tired of their efforts outshining their paychecks.

Second, the industry itself has been changing, specifically in ways that are attractive to professional people. According to Tom Barrett, author of *Dare to Dream, Work to Win*: "Network marketing has reached new levels of integrity, professionalism, mainstream acceptability, levels of profitability, technological sophistication, training and support." Pep rallies and rah-rah conventions have been replaced with online product demonstrations, video presentations, business opportunity meetings and expensive training. These transformations are legitimizing the industry for people who wouldn't otherwise give it the time of day.

So, for those who have what it takes to be successful in other areas of their life, network marketing is a hotbed of opportunity. We're not saying it's Easy Street; we're just saying that for folks with some drive, intelligence and a work ethic, network marketing is one of the simplest ways to earn a living. And accomplished professionals are starting to figure that out.

> There has never been a better time in the history of network marketing. Security is being redefined. The economic landscape has opened the door. With all of the jobs that have been lost and people who need to recreate six-figure incomes as quickly as possible, network marketing is the answer. That is, if they can wrap their brains around the opportunity.
>
> Rod Nichols, Author, Pastor, and Network Marketer

Going Global

Network marketing isn't just popular in the United States. It's really gaining some ground in the rest of the world as well. Today, 65 million people worldwide are registered network marketing distributors, and 58 countries participate in the World Federation of Direct Selling Association. Although the United States has the highest volume of sales from network marketing companies, enormous increases in other countries—some as high as 121% in a five-year period—have been recorded around the world.

Network marketing doesn't have quite the same stigma in other countries it has in the United States, but the economies overseas are still just as fragile. The unemployment rates in Canada, France, Finland, Greece, Portugal and Sweden, for example, are only slightly lower than in the United States, while countries like Ireland, Spain and Slovakia are faring far worse. Japan's unemployment rate, although lower than most, reached a 55-year high in mid-2009. The bigger network marketing companies know this, and have already made their move.

As the door to this industry continues to expand overseas, network marketers will be uniquely poised to blitz right through it.

#11: Recognition for a Job Well Done

Other than a holiday card and some fruitcake, when's the last time you were thanked... *just for doing your job?*

Have you ever gotten flowers on your birthday... *from your boss?* When you have an idea, suggestion or concern to register with your company, are you heard... *by the CEO?* Did the last sentence just make you laugh?

It may sound funny, but it's really quite sad. These days, the average employee is no more than the hired help, working longer and harder than ever before. We know the paycheck is great, but let's face it, you're *human.* You want to feel appreciated. We do, too.

In network marketing, you don't just get paid, you get *recognized.* We're not talking about free trips and prizes, or jewelry and fancy cars (although you get those too). We're talking about *real* acknowledgement—a personal call from the President, a private line to Customer Service, the chance to participate in company decisions, and a "thank you" for a job well done.

When you join a network marketing company, you're not just part of a team; you're a member of a family. Your voice is heard. Your suggestions matter. Your vote is counted. When you meet your numbers, you are *called up* to the stage, *called out* in front of your peers; you are applauded, praised, celebrated. You are loved.

Any takers?

Get the Facts

- According to a survey by CareerBuilder, in 2010 nearly 77% of Americans were living paycheck to paycheck, up from 61% the year before. [vi]

- According to a Gallup poll, 68% of Americans could not cover a $5,000 emergency with cash. [vii]

- The number of bankruptcy filings rose from 1.41 million in 2009 to 1.53 million in 2010, a 9% increase. [viii]

- Total consumer debt has doubled since 1980. [ix]

- Unemployment for lawyers jumped 66% to a 10-year high in 2009. [x]

- In New York City, the number of white-collar workers outside the financial industry receiving unemployment checks in October, 2008 was up by more than 40% from the same month in 2007. The number of college graduates collecting benefits was up by 50%. [xi]

- Approximately 1.1 million jobs in corporate finance, information technology and other business functions were lost at large American and European companies in 2008 and 2009, due to a combination of offshoring, productivity improvements and lack of economic growth. It is estimated that over 1.3 million additional jobs will disappear by 2014. [xii]

- A survey of 245 large American companies in February, 2009 revealed that 6% of respondents surveyed were planning mandatory furloughs between 2009 and 2010, with 11% having already implemented one. [xiii]

Chapter Four

Get With the Times

> A wise man changes his mind.
> A fool never will.
>
> *Spanish Proverb*

So if network marketing is so great, why in the world isn't everyone doing it?

Oh boy, where do we start?

Network marketing is probably about as controversial as politics, and people's opinions of it are just as fierce. The problem is, the majority of those opinions are based in *fiction*, not fact. And often in rumors that are decades old.

So let's cover the main objections about network marketing, and get to the bottom of this grapevine once and for all.

#1: It's a Pyramid Scheme

The instant people hear about network marketing, the first thing out of their mouths is, "*Isn't that one of those pyramid things?*"

For whatever reason, despite the fact that it's a Wonder of the World, when the majority of people think of a pyramid, they think *scam*. It's true. Never before, in the history of our society, have people been so afraid of a triangle.

So, why *is* the word "pyramid" so taboo? After all, most successful organizations are shaped like a pyramid. Our military, government, universities, corporations, hospitals, and school systems: all pyramids. And there's a reason for that. As an organizational structure of hierarchy, it's one of the strongest and most sustainable around. *Pyramids* are good.

Pyramid schemes, however, are not.

Most people think a pyramid scheme is an organization where one person (or a few) sits at the top making all the money, while the masses at the bottom do all the work, right? *Wrong.* That's not a pyramid scheme. *That's the company you work for.* And that's perfectly legal. Think about it, how many employees make more than their managers or CEO?

Legitimate network marketing companies don't look anything like that. In a network marketing company, all people start at the exact same place, but excel at different rates. *Anyone* can make it to the top. For some people, it takes months to get there, for others, it takes years. Some never do. Either way, it has nothing to do with *when* you signed up or *who* referred you. Many of the top earners of network marketing companies are people who got in decades after the company was established, and long after the first person to sign up. More importantly, many are earning far more than the person who referred them.

Say what?

That's right. The biggest misconception about network marketing is that the person who referred you (often called a "sponsor") is in a permanent position to ride your coattails all the way to the bank. But that is entirely false. In almost all network marketing companies, if your efforts outshine your sponsor's, you can pass or leapfrog right over him. That means <u>**you can earn a better title, and a lot more dough.**</u>

Just how is that possible? Well, the answer lies in the pie chart from Chapter Three.

Network marketing companies make a set amount of money per product or service. That means there's only a certain amount of profit to go around. If they had to pay dozens of layers of network marketers, they'd go broke. So at some point, the commissions taper off.

The good news is that the resulting system is totally fair. Your sponsor cannot reach your *entire* network, or profit from *all* of your income. Of course, she will always get some form of compensation, which stands to reason; after all, *she* made the referral. But the only person who can eat all of your pie is *you*.

Got that? Good.

Now, let's look at the difference between a legitimate network marketing company and a pyramid scheme.

Pyramid Scheme: Type One

The first type of pyramid scheme is actually called a Ponzi scheme (named for the criminal who made it famous). It doesn't involve a product, service, or even business at all. It's just a scam described as an investment opportunity.

In a Ponzi scheme, the initial people who invest are paid from the subsequent investments of *other* people who later join the scheme. In other words, no genuine profit is made; the money is earned from brand new, unsuspecting members. Eventually, as the scheme becomes popular (remember, a few people *do* actually make money), the number of people entering the *bottom* of the scheme exceeds the number of people exiting the *top* of the scheme—hence the pyramid shape. The result is significant profit for the people who got in first, and anyone else who rises to the top before the scheme collapses.

With Ponzi schemes, since no business is involved, no real sale is made, and no security is traded, it's considered a scam.

If this is starting to sound familiar, it's because you've probably seen something similar before. Remember the chain letter you got as a kid—the one asking you to send a dollar (or in our case, ladies, a cute new pair of panties) to the person at the top of the list? Same deal. Illegal.

Eventually, Ponzi schemes are discovered and dismantled, which leaves the innocent people at the bottom in a monetary (or lingerie) deficit. The most tragic example of this was the Bernie Madoff scandal—yes, a Ponzi scheme—where thousands of people were defrauded to the tune of $50 billion.

Pyramid Scheme: Type Two

The second type of pyramid scheme is one in which a product or service exists, but is really just a cover for the scam itself. In reality, the products are never actually used. The company makes very little profit from the sale of these goods, but instead derives *almost all* of its revenue from the enrollment fees of new recruits. The representatives get paid the same way—in kick-backs for bringing new people into the scheme, as opposed to sales actually made. In that sense, it's a lot like a Ponzi scheme, but with some meaningless (and often overpriced) products changing hands.

Legitimate Network Marketing Companies

Legitimate network marketing companies are completely different. They sell real products and services that are actually in demand. They do not compensate their network marketers for recruitment *alone*. There are no direct kickbacks from sign-up fees, and reps are only paid when a sale is made to an end user, or personally consumed (we're allowed to buy from ourselves).

Pyramid Schemes	Legitimate NM Companies
Sham products that don't work, or are of little value to consumer. Often overpriced.	Legitimate societal demand for products. Valuable, competitively priced.
Consultant commissions paid purely for recruiting, or direct kickbacks from enrollment fees.	Consultant compensation tied to product/ service distribution and sales.
Large enrollment fees. Big product buy-ins required. Companies and distributors profit from training.	Low start-up costs. Companies and distributors do not derive profit from training.

So as you can see, at a distance, network marketing companies can look similar to pyramid schemes, but up close, they are dramatically different.

The confusion between pyramid schemes and network marketing companies is, in part, what created the stigma of the industry as a whole. That's because, when the network marketing industry was born, it was highly unregulated. Any old scammer could start a company, invent a product, funnel it through a "network marketing" channel, exaggerate product claims, and promise everyone millions, but with nothing to back it up. Unfortunately, that's exactly what many of them did. As a result, they opened and closed their doors in a matter of months, leaving a lot of casualties in their wake.

On top of that, con-artists who didn't have the capital to start their own businesses jumped into existing companies as independent representatives, and immediately began implementing fraudulent schemes of their own, many of which the companies themselves were not aware of. So in sum, there were *slimy* network marketing companies, and *legitimate* network marketing companies with slimy reps. It was the Wild West.

Around this time, our society wasn't sophisticated about these business models, so many otherwise intelligent people took the bait—hook, line and sinker. To make matters worse, the buy-ins to join were generally larger than they are today. That's because, without the Internet, people had to acquire a significant amount of product at the outset in order to have inventory to sell. In other words, when people lost, they lost *big*. The result was that disgruntled reps were left with mountains of product they couldn't unload, debt they couldn't repay, and relationships they couldn't repair. So they did what any decent person would do in that situation—warn all of their friends to stay away.

As a result of the mess, the Federal Trade Commission finally intervened and sued the bigger network marketing companies over a number of issues, including the legitimacy of the business model itself. At the end of the day, the courts declared that network marketing was a *completely legal way of distributing goods*, but the damage was done. A few bad apples had spoiled it for the bunch, and over thirty years later, many people are still not up to date.

Today, the industry has far more regulation than it did thirty years ago. There are trade associations and watchdog groups galore. Problems still exist, but fortunately, most of them are practice-specific and not industry-wide. But, as with anything—the stock market, a franchise, a marriage—you should do your due diligence before you get involved with a network marketing company. Trust us, no one wants more regulation in the network marketing industry than network marketers themselves. If the frauds and shady tactics were eliminated, we'd all have an easier time doing business.

If you're still skeptical, do your research. The Direct Selling Association (www.dsa.org) is a great place to start.

The only thing we ask is that you don't throw the baby out with the bath water. The Bernie Madoff scandal hasn't deterred people from investing in legitimate companies, right? Of course not. They're just digging deeper now before they do it. The same can be said for network marketing—don't let its controversial past cause you to overlook its future potential.

So, let's review. Pyramid = shape. Pyramid scheme = scam. Network marketing = legitimate. You = do your homework.

Are we clear?

#2: You Have to Get in Early to be Successful

We have to admit, it's hard to respond to an objection about network marketing that we don't even understand. But we'll give it a try.

We often hear people say that they are resistant to network marketing, or a particular company, because it's just too late to get in—like they missed some sort of boat that just set sail.

The biggest problem with this myth is that no one is able to define it. For example, how early is early? Three months? Three years? Three decades? In the grand scheme of things, if a company is first to adopt a trend that takes time to catch on in mainstream society, is it possible to ever be too late? What if a company is fifty years old, with a product line that's brand new? Aren't you now ahead of the curve?

You see the dilemma.

Remember, network marketing is slow-growing compared to a Super Bowl commercial; it takes longer than thirty seconds for millions to receive the word. And even if a large percentage of the people have *heard* of a product, that doesn't mean they have *heard about how great it is.* People watch trailers for movies all the time, but often only see the one a friend recommends. The entire world can be aware of a brand, but still not use it.

What we're saying is, early is relative. So unless everyone you've ever met is buying from, or involved with, the *exact same network marketing company*, and you have *no* plans to ever *meet new people* or *make new friends*, congratulations— you're right on time.

By the way, a few words of caution for those of you looking just to get in early. Network marketing companies suffer from the same growing pains as any other start-up or new business; a high percentage of them fold within the first few years. So look out, because when it comes to being an early bird, not everyone gets a worm.

> There's almost no difference in income potential between those who get in early and those who don't. And our society is so diverse that it doesn't really matter. There will always be people who want to take the risk with an unknown brand, hoping for the big reward, and people who want to wait until a company has established its credibility and financial security.
>
> Doris Wood, Founder, MLMIA (Multi-Level Marketing International Association)

#3: Saturation

This conspiracy theory is sort of a hybrid of the "getting in early" and "pyramid scheme" myths. The assumption behind it is that when the market becomes saturated with a particular product, the demand will run out. Or when the market gets saturated with salespeople, there will be a shortage of customers to go around.

Neither of these arguments has any merit, other than on paper. Sure, technically everyone could have a certain type of product, like a mattress, refrigerator or computer. But that doesn't ever eliminate the demand. Products get old;

they need to be renewed, revised and replaced. You don't see Apple discontinuing iPods just because everyone seems to have one. On the contrary, the company just becomes more innovative, inventing newer, better and cuter models of the versions already released.

Network marketing companies are no different. In fact, few of them encounter this issue in the first place, because they *intentionally* get into industries where products need to be reordered. From vitamins to face creams to telephone service—the whole business is designed to bring the user back for more. They're no strangers to innovation, either. You can bet that before a product gets tired, there's a newer, shinier one waiting in the wings.

And we suppose it's *hypothetically* possible for millions and millions of people to join the same network marketing company, but that also never happens. There are hundreds of network marketing companies to choose from; the idea that everyone will join the same one is sort of ludicrous. Besides, the population changes over time. Every day, a whole new crop of people turn eighteen and form a brand new consumer base. At the same time, a population of independent distributors and customers dies off. To suggest that in a short span of time, millions upon millions of people will all choose the same career is completely wild. Not only has that never happened in network marketing, it's never happened *at all*.

Saturation case = closed.

#4: I'm Not Like Those People

The good news is that network marketing is an equal opportunity business. The bad news is that network marketing is an equal opportunity business—*any*one can get in. That's right—no education, degree, diploma, certificate, license, experience, resume, interview, references, IQ or *ounce of class* required. All you need is a pulse and a social security number.

So, given this gigantic welcome mat, it's no surprise that network marketing can be a magnet for misfits, flunkees, sleaze-balls and buffoons. And it's also not shocking that these fools tarnish the industry with their obnoxious (and completely ineffective) tactics once they get in. You know the ones—the innocent happy hour that turns into a sneak-attack business presentation, the person who saturates her Facebook page every hour with product claims and promotions, the cousin who harasses you with samples and turns your family reunion into an infomercial. You're not the only ones who've been victimized by this garbage before. We have, too.

But *wake up*—the fact that network marketing attracts a few weirdos has nothing to do with the legitimacy of the business model itself. More importantly, this fact has nothing to do with *you*.

> When network marketing is done the right way, it's not the same industry as the one most people are criticizing.
>
> Tim Sales, Network Marketing Expert, Author, and Trainer

Thomas Edison once said, "Who you are will show up in what you do." And network marketing is certainly no exception. If you're professional now, you'll be professional in network marketing. If you're cheesy now, you'll be cheesy in network marketing. If you are completely ineffective at life, you will be *completely ineffective* at network marketing. It's not rocket science, people. It's common sense.

Besides, these folks are not just in network marketing, they're in every business. They're just more noticeable in network marketing because it's a business that involves connecting with people. And we hate to break it to you, but if your cousin is acting like a stalker now that he's doing network marketing, that's not a network marketing problem. It's a *family* problem.

Don't let a few fruit loops discourage you from considering a business model that is legitimate and fair. Trust us; you'll find the people who are ethical, smart and fun. We'd love the company.

> This business is not without its share of detractors. And it has had its share of hucksters and flim-flam artists—unethical people trying to make a quick buck. But by its very nature and design, network marketing is a strikingly fair, democratic, socially responsible system of generating wealth.
>
> Robert T. Kiyosaki, Author

#5: It's Insincere

Ahhh… the dreaded kickback. How can we ever be sure that a referral is sincere when money is involved?

The answer is: we can't. It's just a fact of life—some people are genuine, others are not.

It's not like this is breaking news. You didn't really think that movie-star spokeswoman was actually using drugstore make-up, did you? Or that four out of five dentists *really* recommended that gum?

The point is, you're being marketed to every day—every time you log on to the internet, click an affiliate link, watch a commercial or join a referral-based network. Sure, it hurts more when a friend is insincere, but that doesn't mean network marketing is to blame. It means your friend picked the wrong products to represent, and you need to take that up with your friend.

Look, most people involved in network marketing are *sincerely* enthusiastic about the products they represent. In fact, a lot of them *became* reps for a company specifically to get a discount on their favorite products. With hundreds of network marketing companies to choose from, why on Earth would they choose one they didn't like?

Not only do most of them love the products, we can guarantee you they're fired up about the compensation plan as well. With everything we've told you about it so far, can you blame them? If you really loved what a product can do for your life, and you've made a decent income just telling other people about it, wouldn't you be drinking the Kool-Aid, too?

Besides, we've pointed out that most of you already do network marketing anyway; you just didn't know it.

The restaurant, boutique or spa recommendation—that's network marketing. The dentist referral—network marketing. The movie your friends should watch, book they should read, song they should download—network marketing. Every day you spread the word for brands you love. *That's network marketing.*

So listen, if you're going to walk like a duck, act like a duck and quack like a duck, shouldn't you get paid to *be a duck?*

You get the point.

#6: I Don't Have Time

This is by far the most underwhelming argument against network marketing we've ever heard.

There's no such thing as not having enough time for network marketing. If you have time to read this book, you have time for network marketing. If you have time to tell your friends about a restaurant you love, you have time for network marketing. If you have time to complain about your job, you have time for network marketing. If you have time to surf the Internet, watch TV and read the tabloids, you have time for network marketing. If you are so pressed for time that you can't do network marketing, you need a solution that will give you more time. *That* is network marketing.

#7: I Don't Want to Make Money off of My Friends

A lot of people are resistant to network marketing because they don't want to "use their friends." But the stigma of network marketing doesn't come from people *using* their networks. It comes from people *abusing* their networks.

Network marketing isn't about asking your friends to buy products they don't need or spend money they don't have. It isn't about turning every happy hour or dinner party into a business meeting or pitch. It isn't about hounding or harassing time and time again. And if your friend does it that way, he's doing it wrong!

Network marketing is—plain and simple—about sharing things you love with people you suspect will love them, too. It's about asking people to consider redirecting the dollars already headed out the door to something they might like better; something that benefits them *and* you.

This is no different from how it works in any other business or community. If your friend owned a restaurant, would you eat there? Would you be offended if they asked you to try a dish? Of course not. If your friend was performing in a concert, would you buy a ticket? We think you would.

Do you recommend your friends for jobs? Set them up on dates? Sponsor them in charity walks, donate to their causes, or loan them a few bucks? Do they vote for your stuff on Facebook, comment on your blog, shop at your store, frequent your salon and send business your way? Is your freezer full of Girl Scout cookies and fundraiser candy bars? Did you get tax, legal, medical and business advice last year? For *free*?

Okay then. So why, when a friend asks you to try a sample or browse a catalog, are you suddenly so annoyed?

We're not asking you to eat at our restaurant for breakfast, lunch and dinner, or see our show *every* night of the week. We're not asking you to *sustain* us; we're asking you to *support* us. *Just as we'd support you.*

So, if that means we're *using* our friendships, then fine. Guilty as charged.

#8: High Failure Rate

Your friend, your cousin, your colleague, your colleague's cousin's friend—everyone knows someone who "failed" at network marketing.

We're not here to deny the statistics about the success rate of network marketing. They are what they are. But we do want to warn you that while the numbers may not lie, they certainly don't tell the whole story.

So here it is.

Some People Are Not Qualified To Do It

Network marketing may be simple, but it's not always easy. Like any other endeavor worth pursuing—college, graduate school, sports, acting, a military career, etc.—network marketing requires a certain skill set and character. We're talking about ambition, a work ethic, people skills, persistence, patience, a positive attitude, commitment, self-reflection and the willingness to learn. If a person doesn't have these traits, and isn't willing to acquire them, he or she will *not* succeed at network marketing.

Sadly, most of the people who join network marketing companies *just to get rich quick* don't have these qualities. That's how they ended up doing network marketing to begin with—they weren't *qualified* for anything else. So don't be fooled by the numbers. These people would lower the success rate of *any* industry; network marketing is just the one that let them in.

Besides, have you ever done the research on just how many people in America have graduate degrees, reach top military positions, own successful businesses after five years, play professional sports, or make over $100,000 per year? Okay then. The world is full of people who don't have or do what it takes to make it to the top. Network marketing is no different.

People Quit Too Soon

Second, the only way to truly fail in network marketing is to quit. And the majority of people quit way too soon.

Network marketing attracts a lot of folks expecting to become the next rags to riches story, and they want to cash in *yesterday*. So they get involved in the business, discover that it actually takes time and work to make money, and then quit. When they do, they tell the whole world that network marketing doesn't work.

Network marketing *does* work. It just didn't work for *them*.

People who are looking to get something for nothing are common in network marketing. And they're more likely to blame the industry, rather than their lack of effort or skills, for their failures. They've done it in every aspect of their life—diets, marriages, careers—the list goes on.

Like starting a business, going to college or entering a challenging profession, it can take months or even years before the investments in network marketing really pay off. That's because, by their nature, networks take time to grow. The progress builds over time, and the most dramatic success occurs at the *end*, not the beginning. The exercise on the next page will help you understand why.

Understanding the Growth Pattern of Network Marketing

The Million Dollar Question: Would you rather have $1 million today, or one penny, doubled each day for 30 days?

The majority of people would rather have $1 million, because they don't understand the concept of exponential growth. As you can see in the adjacent diagram, just like a network marketing business, it takes time for multiplication to yield significant results. In the beginning, the results don't look very impressive. *But the math doesn't lie.* Eventually, the reward becomes substantial.

This is why people who quit network marketing too soon never reap the benefits of their initial efforts. Their short-term blindness prevents them from seeing the long-term vision. They feel under-compensated in the beginning, and don't wait to be overcompensated in the end. In network marketing, you can work hard for a *short* time, so that you don't have to work hard for a *long* time.

Day	Value
0	$ 0.01
1	$ 0.02
2	$ 0.04
3	$ 0.08
4	$ 0.16
5	$ 0.32
6	$ 0.64
7	$ 1.28
8	$ 2.56
9	$ 5.12
10	$ 10.24
11	$ 20.48
12	$ 40.96
13	$ 81.92
14	$ 163.84
15	$ 327.68
16	$ 655.36
17	$ 1,310.72
18	$ 2,621.44
19	$ 5,242.88
20	$ 10,485.76
21	$ 20,971.52
22	$ 41,943.04
23	$ 83,886.08
24	$ 167,772.16
25	$ 335,544.32
26	$ 671,088.64
27	$ 1,342,177.28
28	$ 2,684,354.56
29	$ 5,368,709.12
30	$ 10,737,418.24

← start with a penny.

Now is probably when you're thinking you should have taken the million bucks. Don't fret. Looks can be deceiving.

← Don't quit now! You're closer than you think.

← Wait for it...

Jackpot!
Delayed gratification pays off.

We know this won't stop people from treating network marketing as a quick fix, or feeling cheated when they're still broke after a few weeks. But at the risk of sounding like a broken record, the fact that these people have failed has *nothing to do with you*. Like we said, these are some of the most financially unsuccessful people in the world. They wouldn't recognize delayed gratification if it punched them in the face. They are the same people who think the Lotto is a valid retirement plan and expect Ed McMahon to knock on their door. The fact that they have unrealistic expectations about network marketing, or are the first to buy into obvious hype, isn't out of the ordinary for these people. It's par for the course.

So yes, there are casualties in network marketing. But there are no victims.

Most people don't achieve significant financial wealth [in network marketing]. That's because they don't define specific goals and make the necessary commitment of time and energy to achieve them.

Dr. Charles W. King, Author and Professor of Network Marketing

What Constitutes Failure?

The real problem with trying to calculate how many people have failed at network marketing is that there is no agreed-upon definition of failure. There are all different types of stories in network marketing—some that might be classified as failure to one, and success to another.

For example, there are people in network marketing making only meager amounts of money because their networks are new and small. The larger paychecks are in the not-too-distant future. Are *they* failures? There are also people who aren't even in network marketing for the money. They do it for the camaraderie, the community support, the personal development and—above all—the discounts! They're happy right where they are. Are *they* failures? And there are people who decided to give network marketing a whirl, or try their luck to see if they could achieve overnight success. They didn't, and so they quit. Are *they* failures? Or are they just quitters?

What we're saying is, it's obviously impossible to take a snapshot of the network marketing industry and reach any conclusive results about its success rate. And even if you do, what's that got to do with you?

The realistic people know that success in network marketing isn't about chance or luck. It's not about hedging your bets based on what other people have or haven't done. Network marketing is about rolling the dice on *yourself.* So you tell us, are those good odds?

Flip-Flop CEO Stories

Stacey Bean, M.D. Flip-Flop CEO
BS, Biology, and MA in Exercise Physiology
Board Certification in Emergency Medicine
Network Marketer

My husband and I were Emergency Physicians for over 7 years. We worked hard and followed society's prescription for success. We went to college, graduated top of our class in medical school, and had successful careers. We worked nights, weekends and holidays, and with two small children, we became two ships passing in the night. As I watched my children getting closer to school age, I was torn because they were going to be in school Monday through Friday while my husband and I worked nights. Feeling overwhelmed, I tearfully told my husband "if this is success, you can have it." We had stopped dreaming and were just surviving.

We were passionate about making a difference in the lives of others through medicine; however, it was at the sacrifice of our own family. We were looking for something that would allow us more time together and more choices. I never thought that I would find that opportunity in Network Marketing.

Initially skeptical, I had multiple excuses such as having no time, not wanting to "sell" to my friends and not knowing anybody. I also couldn't get over the thought that I was "above" this business. However, my friend said something that I couldn't get out of my head: "If you keep doing what you're doing, where will you be in five years?" My husband encouraged me to take a look. What I found left me with the attitude of, "Who *wouldn't* want to do this business?!" I saw a Plan B that I could build alongside my current job, and I jumped in so that my husband and I could someday have options to live the life we had dreamed of, instead of dreaming about the life we did not have. I didn't realize that "someday" would never come for us.

In May of 2008, I awoke to my worst nightmare. I received a phone call that the MedFlight Helicopter that my husband was working on as the flight physician had crashed and there were no survivors. In the blink of an eye, my life crashed down around me. Everything I had dreamed of—my soul mate, the father of my children, the person I wanted to grow old with, travel with, do medical mission trips with, and raise our children with—was gone. I spent the next four months trying to piece back together what was left of our lives. I realized that if I went back to medicine and continued trading time for money, I couldn't replace both of our incomes, and my children, who had just lost their dad, would also lose their mom to a full-time job. I have become acutely aware, given the sudden loss of my husband, that if something happened to me, my employer would not provide for my children when I am gone. However, since my business is willable, I'm building an ongoing legacy for my kids.

Today, I'm able to choose to stay home with my kids and be fully present in their lives. My time is managed by me. My decision to leave medicine was not as difficult as you may think. It's a gift to have the freedom of choice to fit my career around my family. I don't know of any other profession that could give me the same "dual physician" income while raising my kids as a single mom.

My husband and I had a vision of making the world a better place one person at a time. Now, I am able to continue to make a difference in the lives of others, but no longer at the expense of my family.

Stacey's Words of Wisdom

Believe that you have choices. This business has been the lighthouse in my storm. No matter what life throws at you, choose to live your dreams, even when you have to learn to dance in the rain. Work your business with integrity and compassion and believe in the possibilities. Life is too short to wait until someday.

Monica Gray, Flip-Flop CEO
BS, Kinesiology
Certified Personal Trainer
Network Marketer

I followed the traditional American path, earning a degree in Kinesiology and becoming a Certified Personal Trainer.

My original plan was to build a network of other trainers so that I could have some leverage and time for my young triplets. But with my family's hectic schedule, that would have been very hard to manage. Although I was passionate about the industry, and knew I would love the work, I was resistant to the amount of effort it would take.

Two years ago, a friend introduced me to a network marketing company that was a good fit for my passion of health and fitness. I'd turned my back on the industry for years—probably for the same reasons as a lot of other people—but this time I listened. My triplets were four years old at the time, and I needed a more flexible plan.

Today, I'm retired, thanks to my network marketing paychecks. In fact, my business has grown 200% in the last six months alone. There's no stable of personal trainers, and no large business to oversee. Now we go to Disneyland in the middle of the week, we extend our vacations if we feel like it, we have no debt, and a growing savings account.

The best part is that, last month, my husband was able to officially retire too. He has worked so hard all these years, and although he absolutely loved his job, he loves being home with us more. To be able to have the cushion to help him quit working, and stay home with our family, is the greatest blessing of all time.

Although I don't have a traditional business, I actually think that network marketing is entrepreneurial in its own way. It's not about re-inventing the wheel or doing anything new, but how people grow their businesses and whether they become successful depends a lot on their approach to marketing, their personality traits and their outlook, which is the same in entrepreneurship. People think it is very cookie cutter and all about blending in, but it's not. There are a million different ways to do this business.

Network marketing was definitely the answer for my life. My only regret is not doing it sooner. If I had, we would be richer. Simple as that.

Monica's Words of Wisdom

People that say they don't have time to do this business are precisely the people that need to do it! This business, when done right, will give you the luxury of time you so desperately want. I'm living proof of that.

Jo Ann Calvin, Flip-Flop CEO
BS, Business Management
Former Government Employee
Network Marketer

Before network marketing, I was the quintessential government worker. I had a secure job as a Trainer with the Department of Transportation, and was content to earn a steady paycheck.

When I first learned of network marketing, I was just happy to use the products. In fact, my sponsor took me to over four years-worth of company meetings before the thought even crossed my mind to do the business. The turning point was after a meeting, when a fellow network marketer casually mentioned the amount of her recent paycheck. She'd made more in that month than most make in a year. I decided right then and there that, if she could make that much money, I could make a few hundred a month. My expectations were low.

They say that every three months, something changes in a woman's life, and that month something definitely changed in mine. I'd always had enough money to get by, enough to pay the bills, and maybe a little extra. But suddenly, out of the blue, I realized that I deserve more. So I jumped in.

Of course, over time I set my sights a little higher. I was starting to discover the magnitude of what I had in front of me, and the potential for freedom. In an instant, that became my passion—helping other people to find that freedom.

I built my network marketing business alongside my job at the DOT. I worked it about 10 hours a week, with four kids and a husband. Within one year (or even less), I was making a salary equal to—or slightly more than—my full-time job. But I still didn't quit. In fact, by the time I gave my notice, I was earning roughly three times that amount and had gotten two free cars. But I was afraid to abandon the security. More than that, I was afraid to give up my power. It seems funny to say now, but I loved the dressing up, the going to work with a briefcase, and wearing my power suit to meetings. It seemed so strong, powerful and important. But network marketing made me realize that power comes from within. Today, I sit at Starbucks sipping my coffee while I watch other people play the corporate game. It's no longer for me.

I love what this business has done for my life, and I'm proud of the fact that I'm one of the foremost African American Sales Directors for my company. More importantly, I love what it can do for other people. Anytime I hear from someone who is just discovering the excitement in building this business, I'm thrilled. I love seeing the change, especially in women, when they realize they can do it; when they step outside of their comfort zone, into a new reality—a reality that they love.

Jo Ann's Words of Wisdom

If you think this business doesn't work, then sign up and challenge the company by doing everything they tell you to, for one year. Prove that you can't make as much money as you're making right now. That's how you'll succeed.

Jeff Van Blaricum, Flip-Flop CEO
Network Marketer

I was introduced to network marketing when I was in high school. My older brother had gotten involved with a brand new company and was already quite successful, so I decided to join him. Unfortunately, that company didn't have an established track record and went belly-up. So I found another one, but the same thing happened again. Although I was frustrated, I never gave up. I knew the business model worked; I just needed a solid company and some good mentorship.

During this time, I was doing odd jobs and trying my hand at self-employment. I'd always had an entrepreneurial spirit, so I opted not to go to college and try to earn some money instead. At that time, that meant working in a tire shop for $10 an hour.

The job wasn't bad for a young kid my age; it just wasn't where I wanted my life to lead.

Eventually I found the right network marketing company. The very first check I received was more than I was earning at the tire store, so I quit and never looked back. I've been with that company for twenty years, although I've been retired for the last ten. In fact, the majority of the people I introduced to the business are retired too, still drawing paychecks for their up-front work. It's a complete myth that only one person makes all the money.

In fact, the earning potential in this industry is far greater than people realize. That's because the subject of network marketing is not taught in schools. People underestimate the potential for residual income; they think it only exists in entertainment and publishing. They look at network marketing and think it's too good to be true. But in reality, many of the nation's millionaires have come from this industry.

Recently, however, I've noticed the tides changing with the recession. People are getting kicked around more in life and in society. They are starting to realize the limitations of their chosen path—namely trading time for money, which has a cap. You can only go so far with that. So they're taking a second look at what we do. It's time for another growth spurt for network marketing. It's a very exciting time.

Jeff's Words of Wisdom

Just like anything worthwhile, network marketing takes work, effort and energy. But the difference is that, in network marketing, the work, effort and energy can compensate you for years to come. Like I always say, "If you'll do for a few years what others aren't willing to do, you can live the rest of your life like others only dream of."

Margaret and Steve Ruby, Flip-Flop CEOs

Bachelor of Arts, Teaching Credential
Network Marketers

My husband and I had quite a few careers before getting involved in network marketing. At a young age, I got my teaching credential, and taught kindergarten for a few years. I later started my own consulting business in the personal development field, and went on to write my own curriculum, as well as a bestselling book. My husband was a pioneer in the video industry, had owned multiple different franchises, and was working on a new invention related to sound therapy. We figured we had seen and done it all.

Unfortunately, as the economy started to take a downturn, our businesses began to suffer. We had no idea what we were going to do if it didn't bounce back. So we went looking for a way to re-invent ourselves. We were both 62 at the time.

Shortly thereafter, I was contacted by a former student who introduced me to an anti-aging product that I fell in love with. I immediately told all of my friends about it, and right away, people started spreading the word. Although I knew the product came from a network marketing company, I didn't consider myself to be a network marketer, nor did I want to be one. I had some very negative opinions about the industry that came from my involvement with a few of them years before. So I didn't share the business model with friends at all. I hadn't even read the compensation plan!

Before I knew it, I had gotten my second paycheck from all the product purchases coming in, and I realized that I should probably take the business seriously. My husband agreed. So we flew to the company headquarters to check it out. We wanted to see what kind of depth was behind the company, and what their financial track record was like. We were impressed. At that point, we dove right in. Today, three years later, we work the business together.

We've had tremendous success with this company and have achieved our dreams of financial security once and for all. Not only are we making more than we ever did with our respective businesses, we also have one of the fastest growing teams in the company. Talk about re-inventing ourselves!

The best part about this business is the number of people we've been able to help. A lot of Baby Boomers are going through huge financial crises. The industries they've been trained in for so long are suffering. We are so thankful that we have been shown another way, and are able to share it with our friends. It is incredibly rewarding to see people's lives change right before your eyes.

This industry is great for people our age. It allows them to bring all of the skills they've acquired throughout life and put them to good use. Baby Boomers don't need to throw their lives away because they've lost money or their pension plans. Everything they've done up to this point is an asset to a network marketing business. They are very valuable in this profession.

Network marketing is completely different from the traditional business world. Here, you share your secrets with everyone; you don't hold anything back. There's no competition. It's all about creating community, capitalizing on team strengths and compensating for weaknesses. Every day we are a part of a team effort. I've never had that level of partnership before. It's very comforting. I wish I would have recognized the strength of this industry when I was 20.

Margaret's Words of Wisdom

People think network marketing is "alternative" compared to the traditional environments they're in. In actuality, this business model is more solid than anything else around.

Leanne Grechulk, Flip-Flop CEO
BS, Biomedical Toxicology, MBA
Entrepreneur
Network Marketer

I got involved in network marketing without even knowing it. When I was 24, my personal trainer put me on some wellness products to support my rigorous training schedule. I quickly fell in love with them, and began to order them online on a regular basis. At the time, I had no idea I could earn a living off of my health program, much less help others do the same.

About five years later, I was still using the products. By this time, I had gotten my MBA and was working in Marketing and Customer Relations Management for a large pharmaceutical company. I was searching for a way to become my own boss, although I was unsure how to make it happen. Since I was single and had no start-up cash, I began searching for a plan.

Within a few months I started dating a wonderful guy who, coincidently, was taking the same products

I was, but also building a successful business as an independent associate of the company. He showed me how my desire to help others, and passion for wellness could create the business I was looking for. It was a no-brainer to join (even though everyone around me warned me not to).

Originally I had no plans to build a large team, but that didn't last long because I quickly saw the income potential, and set my sights on financial freedom. A year later, I had enough money to live and quit my corporate job. Today, many of my corporate friends— the ones who used to care about their titles and companies they worked for—are all starting to show interest. Times have changed; network marketing is becoming somewhat of a trend now.

I eventually did start my own business, and authored a bestselling book. And although I'll always be an entrepreneur, because I'm passionate about what I do, I couldn't have gotten here without network marketing.

Part of my business is coaching and mentoring women entrepreneurs. Sadly, so many of them are working their tails off for years and still making less than the equivalent of minimum wage. I tell them network marketing is the smartest decision they can make.

Leanne's Words of Wisdom

I want a business that can hold itself together while I leave for six months. Network marketing is that business.

The Yparrea Family, Flip-Flop CEOs

Steven Yparrea, Donna Yparrea, Matthew Yparrea, Stephanie Yparrea-Budd, Bianca Yparrea-Badger

Steven Yparrea

I went to my very first network marketing presentation for one reason—to prevent my daughters from signing up for something they'd later regret. They'd been hearing about network marketing from a fellow family member, and were on their way to check it out.

Despite the fact that I was in desperate need of a vehicle for time freedom, I wasn't open to network marketing. I always thought it was too good to be true. In retrospect, it wasn't because I didn't believe in the model; it was because I was *afraid* to believe in it.

To say that my mind was changed at that meeting would be an understatement. The presentation blew me away, and I signed up that very night.

At the time, I was working as a Sales Specialist for a large company with a lot of new construction clients. As that industry began to decline in late 2005 and 2006, my company started doing rounds and rounds of lay-offs. Eventually, I was the last one standing. Although I was relieved to still have a job, I was now getting paid the same salary for three times the amount of work. I lived like that for two years, in a constant state of exhaustion and stress.

Like a lot of Baby Boomers, I thought I'd done everything right. Our age group was taught to go to school, get good grades, get set up with a great company, enjoy a few vacations and retire comfortably. But all that's gone now in this strange, emerging world. There's an entire generation of people who did everything they were told. They did nothing wrong, but they have nothing to show for it. It's a real tragedy.

Today, thanks to network marketing, I'm not only retired from my old work, but I have my old self back. I'm 57 going on 30 because of this business. And I plan on getting even younger!

On top of that, I can leave my network marketing business to my family in my will. That's such a huge perk that I wouldn't have gotten at my old job. It's important for me to know that my wife will be able to continue living the lifestyle she's accustomed to after I'm gone. Network marketing has given me that peace of mind. The bonuses in this business are just endless.

Stephanie Yparrea-Budd

Before network marketing came into our lives, we hardly ever saw my dad. Here he was, in his mid-50s, thinking he could slow down as he approached his retirement years, and suddenly he was working harder than ever before. He wasn't able to spend much time with his grandchildren, and my mom was working full-time as well.

So, when we decided to do network marketing as a family, we devised a plan to structure our team in a way that allowed my mom and dad to benefit the most, and hopefully retire off of our collective efforts. It worked. Less than 11 months later, my dad quit his job. My mom works part-time now, only because she still loves her job. There's nothing more satisfying than knowing I helped my parents enjoy their golden years. They deserve it.

The three of us children have benefited from network marketing as well. My husband is in the real estate industry, and we have small children to support. Network marketing has become our saving grace in this horrible housing market. Our entire family has a network marketing success story, but the best part is that we get to see each other all the time. We are finally the family that works together and plays together.

Steven's Words of Wisdom

Our education system is outdated. Young students aren't taught how to be entrepreneurs or think outside the box. We can't continue to allow people to rely on a model that doesn't work. Network marketing is a model that does.

Stephanie's Words of Wisdom

Many people put their dreams on the back burner once they enter the adult world, especially after they have kids. Network marketing allows you to dream again.

Lisa DeMayo, Flip-Flop CEO

BS, Communication Arts
Business Owner, Master Coach
Network Marketer

When I discovered my current network marketing company, I had just gone back to work after having kids. I was making great money in pharmaceutical sales, but had two kids in daycare and was racing the clock like a lunatic. One day I turned to my husband and said, "Is this as good as it gets? We're just going to keep following the rat's tail in front of us, being unfulfilled and answering to someone else?"

Within a week we were at a friend's barbecue, and I noticed a few of her company's products around the house. So I asked her about the business. Can you imagine? She handed me some literature on the top performers in the company, and I was instantly sold. My husband said I was crazy, and didn't have enough time to do it. I didn't care. I immediately got down to business.

Within the first few weeks, dozens of people not only rejected me, but also told me I would fail. I found that to be odd, since they had no real education about the industry, and no idea what they were even saying "no" to. Not one of them had a solution to my current situation, or anything better to offer. Some of my closest contacts even tried to stop me from talking about it. They told me I should "…go to a department store and squirt people with perfume to make more steady money."

But I was undeterred. I was at such a low point in my life—running in circles and not enjoying my life—that the more people rejected me, the more determined I became. So I found someone in the company who'd gotten to where I wanted to go and copied everything she did. Within 75 days, I'd quit my job, substantially increased my income, and earned a brand new car. And this was with a company that was already 25 years old, and a sponsor that lived five hours away. During this time, I even gave birth to our third child. It can be done. I'm proud to say that the initial people who signed up with me are still here today, at the top of the company as well.

Today, my family and friends have come around, not because of how much money I'm making, but because I'm happy, passionate and excited. I'm more fun to be around without the stress of work. Most importantly, they see how many lives I'm changing through network marketing.

I know people who are so overworked that they think a relaxing day involves taking a nap on Saturday, or heading to the beach on the weekends. I can do that any day I want. I wake up when I'm done sleeping, not because it's time to. I eat when I'm hungry, not because it's 12:00. I "get" to do that. Too many people are living a "have to" life. I am living a "get to" life. That's the beauty of network marketing.

Today, I focus my energies on personal development work and being a life and leadership coach, which is my first love. Network marketing has made all of that possible.

Lisa's Words of Wisdom

Network marketing is a "sifting" business, not a "convincing" business. I'm not in it to persuade anyone of the value of this business model. There are enough people out there who will know it when they see it.

Romi Neustadt, Flip-Flop CEO
BA, Journalism and Political Science, Juris Doctor
Network Marketer

I took a rather circuitous route to network marketing. After graduating from college and earning my law degree, I enjoyed a successful career as a trial attorney for three years. While I loved aspects of trial work, the adversarial nature of the profession began to take its toll. So I quit my job, packed my things and moved to New York City to pursue my second career—marketing and public relations.

For twelve years, I was an agency executive in New York and Seattle. I worked hard, and won awards for the communications programs I designed for Fortune 500 companies, international nonprofits and entertainment clients.

All of that changed when my husband and I discovered we were having our first baby. I'd grown up in Montana, and wanted to give my children the gift of the small-town childhood I had. So we decided to take the plunge and move "back home." I left my job and started my own PR consulting firm, while my husband grew his medical practice from our new locale.

For a while, it was nice to be self-employed. I was able to plan my days around my son's schedule, and still maintain my high-profile status in the PR and marketing worlds. But when I had my second child, this time a daughter, I had an epiphany about what my next career would be.

Although our businesses were thriving—I was a nationally recognized PR consultant, while my husband was a nationally recognized physician—we were still facing the same fate that millions of other people face—we couldn't get ahead. By the time we were done paying for the student loans, the Montessori school, the mortgage and the bills, we couldn't fully fund our retirement accounts or the kids' college funds, let alone something extra for the life of adventure we'd always dreamed of. So I went looking for something else, although I didn't yet know what.

Around that time, a PR client of mine who was launching a fantastic jewelry line told me she'd funded her entire business from the earnings of a new network marketing company. When I found out which company she was with, I looked into it, and jumped right in.

Prior to that, I didn't have an opinion on network marketing one way or another. I was always too focused on my other careers to give it a thought. But when I saw the financial freedom it brought my client, I immediately knew it could do the same for me. That was 20 months ago. Today, I'm at the top of that company.

There are so many reasons why I love network marketing. First, my life is no longer governed by the billable hour. Instead, I make a multi-six-figure income off the hours of thousands of individual people. And I, in turn, help them do the same. But although the money and all the other perks are great, it's not the best part. The best part about network marketing is that it allows me to touch people's lives, to help them achieve their goals and become better versions of themselves. And that's what they do for me.

Romi's Words of Wisdom

I'm not at the top of my company because I'm a lawyer or former PR consultant. I'm at the top because I'm 100% coachable and I'm hungry. It doesn't matter what skill set you have when you begin. No one is born knowing how to do this business. You just have to be willing to learn it.

Judy O'Higgins, Flip-Flop CEO
Masters in Social Work
Network Marketer

Before I discovered network marketing, I was a therapist non-stop for 25 years. I worked in a variety of different capacities—from running an alcohol and drug rehabilitation program to starting my own private practice. While I loved my job, eventually I got burnt out on it, which is common in the counseling industry. It's very emotionally rewarding but can also be draining.

I was introduced to network marketing in the mid-1990's by a colleague who was doing social work. Had she not been the one to bring the opportunity to me, I probably wouldn't have listened. I had a negative impression of business in general, having grown up in the 60's and 70's, and I just wanted to help people. But once I really understood the business of network marketing—that we get paid to help others succeed, which is "win-win," as opposed to the dog-eat-dog model of Corporate America—I loved it and jumped right in.

I ultimately had some success with that first network marketing company, but because I wasn't excited about the product, my passion for the business sort of fizzled. Then the company folded. Although I was only working the business part-time, I was very disappointed. I had placed a lot of my hopes on it securing my retirement. At that point, I took a look around and realized that I didn't have an exit plan. I would have to work until my 70s just to support myself. But I knew I didn't have the mental or physical energy to do that. I became very anxious and depressed about the state of my affairs, and I prayed for a solution.

Three months later, the phone rang and it was a gentleman who was a well-known member from my previous network marketing company. He was an amazing trainer and I'd always wanted to be on his team. He introduced me to his new company.

Immediately, I knew it was a fit. I loved the product and service. It was fun. It was something I could stay excited about. More importantly, it was something that had a positive impact on other people's lives. When he agreed to be my coach, I signed up on the spot. I was 60 years old at the time, and taking a leap of faith into another new business.

Within two years, I was able to match my counseling income and retire after all. It's been a real blessing. Today, network marketing is all I do. It actually allows me to utilize a lot of my skills from counseling, and touch people's lives, but in a different way.

Prior to network marketing, I didn't understand the concept of leverage. I thought I had gotten it right by becoming self-employed, but I was still trading time for money. Residual income is a brilliant concept that, along with leverage, makes network marketing an incredible choice.

As one of the first Baby Boomers, I grew up being anti-establishment—not wanting to work for "the man." Of course, things changed and that's exactly what I did for a short period of time. But network marketing has brought all of that full circle for me. Today, I get to help people break free from the constraints of the corporate system, and become their own boss. Now they don't have to take orders or be controlled. It's a completely different type of freedom—one that I'm lucky to have found.

Judy's Words of Wisdom

For the average person, network marketing is the best shot we have to create financial freedom. You can get started in a business for less than the cost of a car payment. The concepts of leverage and residual income can change your life.

Valerie Aloisio, Flip-Flop CEO
Entrepreneur
Network Marketer

After studying Business Administration and a successful career in the corporate world (management training and development for a large liquor company), I discovered entrepreneurship and particularly, network marketing. I instantly recognized it as a viable business opportunity.

After 16 years with my company, my position in the corporate home office was eliminated. My choices after that were few, and relocating to another position or new job was not an option. Since I was 38, a single mom and going through a divorce, I did not want to uproot my children, and I needed something that would allow me to spend more time at home with my kids, and maintain consistency in their lives. Because I had always worked for somebody else, I didn't know how, but I wanted to find something of my own that

I could create and build. Network marketing turned out to be it.

The second I announced my decision to start my own business in network marketing, my family and friends tried to deter me. They had the mentality that going to school, getting a degree, getting a job and working your job was the way to "do life." But I'd done that, and I knew otherwise. More importantly, I wasn't about to make a judgment call about an industry I knew little about. So I immersed myself in the education and training necessary to reach a decision for myself. That was ten years ago.

Thanks to network marketing, I've been able to purchase a nice home for my family in a great area of town and have a great quality of life. I've been fortunate enough to be able to work the business as much as I feel is necessary for the moment. It's important for me to earn a living, but without throwing everything else off balance. Being there for my children is my priority and to find a business that

I could add to our lives, without sacrificing family time, was an incredible thing.

Today, my son is starting his senior year at college, and my daughter is graduating from high school, and going away to school. Welcome to Empty Nest Syndrome! That means Mom is ready to take this business to the next plateau.

Valerie's Words of Wisdom

Network marketing is about putting in the time and effort that's relevant for the life you want. Only you can decide what that is.

Adrian Eimerl, Flip-Flop CEO
BS, Genetics
Network Marketer

By the time I graduated from college with a degree in Genetics, I'd spent $50,000 on my education and had a job offer for $29,000. As hard as I tried, there was no way I could make that math work. Around that time, I met a guy who would later become a great mentor, and he introduced me to the concept of network marketing.

As a young 20-something guy fresh out of college, I did network marketing just to pay the bills. Then I started to have more success, and I became even more motivated—this time by all the material goods my paycheck could buy. Eventually, after I got married and had kids, I discovered the real value of network marketing—the freedom to be with the people I love.

Unlike a lot of people who discover network marketing after they've been burned by some job, I've been a professional networker since the second I joined the "real world." For ten years, I've been living the life of my dreams. I don't even know what it's like to live any other way.

One of the unexpected bonuses of network marketing is how it has transformed me as a person and leader. I started out in this business as a kid, completely untrained. But because I was coachable and willing to learn the system, I'm now a top trainer in my company and a regular speaker at our national conventions. I'm not sure I'd be getting these opportunities anywhere else.

Sure, I've dealt with rejection, and criticism for doing network marketing, but it doesn't affect me. No one rejection is stronger than my desire to provide for my family.

Adrian's Words of Wisdom

Rejection is a part of anything in life. The yes's built my business, but the no's built my character.

Lyndi Eimerl, Flip-Flop CEO
BA, Economics
Entrepreneur
Network Marketer

I got into network marketing in college, when my boyfriend (now husband) and I were looking for some extra income. When I first started out, people laughed at me. At first, the rejection was hard to bear; and my response to it was to shy away from my closest contacts, and work with the people who were mere acquaintances. After a while, however, I realized that if I bought into someone's opinion of what I was doing, I had to buy into their lifestyle and choices. But none of these people had anything I wanted.

I quickly realized that if I wanted certain things, I would have to follow the people who had them, not the ones who didn't.

In addition, I started to feel guilty about building this amazing lifestyle with my husband and keeping it a secret from everyone else. I felt like I was hiding the winning Lotto numbers from the people I loved. So I went back to my close contacts and let them decide for themselves. If they rejected me, that was okay. My obligation to share in the riches was fulfilled.

What I love about network marketing is that it's a teaching and training business, not a sales business. It's about working together with a select group of people to achieve a common goal. Once you do it once, you just have to duplicate it. It's a system that works.

I tried entrepreneurship for a while. My sister and I started a custom handbag line that was a real labor of love. But after a while, it became more labor than love. We did it for three years and saw no real results. But with network marketing, I have a built-in infrastructure that is instantly gratifying, with a lot less work or heartache. We ultimately closed the handbag company because I realized that the best opportunity was already right in front of me.

Lyndi's Words of Wisdom

Regardless of professional status or background, if you have a work ethic, a burning desire for more in life, and you're coachable... you WILL succeed at network marketing.

Christa Jean MacLellan, Flip-Flop CEO
Entrepreneur
Diploma, Design
Network Marketer

By the time I was 18, I knew I wanted to work for myself. I tried network marketing with a variety of different companies, but none of them seemed to fit. Consequently, I had a string of failures under my belt and a seriously sour taste in my mouth about the industry in general. I decided the only way to work for myself was to own a traditional business. A few years later, I launched my fashion blog.

As an entrepreneur and well-known blogger, people thought I was really successful. I'd received a ton of press, gained thousands of followers, interviewed celebrities and hosted some of the most high-profile events in town. But I knew I was missing a piece to the business puzzle because I wasn't making a lot of money, and I was also running around like a crazy person. So while I thought I was successful, my bank account told me otherwise.

When I was approached again about network marketing by a fellow entrepreneur, I was against it. Not only did it not work for me the first time, I was now tied to the "entrepreneur" label. I wasn't sure what being in network marketing would do to my image. But I had a choice to make—either throw in the towel on my business completely and get a day job, or give network marketing another try. I was pushed against the wall. And thank God I was. It was a recipe for success. Today, two years later, my network marketing business is my primary income. It's allowed my fiancée and me to buy our first house, and me to be a stay-at-home mom. Now, my fashion business is just a really great bonus.

Christa Jean's Words of Wisdom

To be successful, to develop character and leadership skills, enroll in network marketing. It's a university you get paid to attend.

Donna Johnson, Flip-Flop CEO
Non-Profit Founder
Network Marketer

When I launched my network marketing business, I was a newly single mom with three kids, and no child support. My options were few. I didn't want to re-enter the work force; I didn't want a Plan B. In retrospect, my lack of options was a blessing in disguise.

Since I had no choice but to go "all in" with my network marketing business, that's exactly what I did. My efforts paid off; I rose almost to the top of the company within four months, and never looked back. That was over twenty years ago.

At the time, the perception of network marketing was more negative than it is today, although I wasn't even aware of it. I think people were just confused because the business model didn't fit the traditional corporate structure. But everything about this business is really quite positive. This business is about *adding value* to others. It's revolutionized the way people, women in particular, feel about themselves. It changes your self-esteem and your sense of self-worth. It allows you to write your own story.

Perhaps the greatest blessing this industry has given me is the ability to give back. My monthly income is now what I used to dream my yearly income would be, so there's a lot to spread around. The more successful you become in network marketing, the more significant your contribution can be. Everyone sees need in the world. We read articles about it, and see videos about it every day on TV. You want to participate. You want to help. This business gives you the abundance with which to do it.

I started my own non-profit several years ago when I was inspired by a need that arose in my family. Today, that non-profit is my life's work. I travel almost year-round, doing what I love—making a difference. It may sound cliché but it's true, when your tank is full, it can't help but overflow out of you and onto others. Network marketing can help fill your tank.

Donna's Words of Wisdom

Trust me, when it comes to helping people, you can do a lot more with money than without it.

Diane Ryan, Flip-Flop CEO
BA, Business and Marketing
Network Marketer

I signed up with a network marketing company just to get the products. My sponsor and I laugh today about the fact that I told her at least five times that I wanted nothing to do with the business.

My life changed when I started to realize that my Corporate America job was becoming dysfunctional. I was burnt out on suits, heels, meetings and travel. I was looking for something more fun. So, if you can believe it, in my early 40s I went back to school to become a hairdresser! Had a "wild hair" day, I say! At the time I figured being a hairdresser would be the change I desperately sought. Today, I believe it was merely part of the path that would eventually lead me to something greater.

I quickly realized the limitation of that path; being a hairdresser is a lot harder than it looks. So, since I was already making so many product referrals to the network marketing company I was with, I decided to "officially" do the business. I was 51 at the time. And some of my first clients were from the salon.

My husband initially had some reservations about my involvement in a network marketing business. That stemmed from an incident 15-20 years ago when one of his best friends called him out of the blue and invited him to dinner. Of course, it was the stereotypical white board meeting that he didn't expect. He was pretty soured from that point on.

But this time around, it was the money that made him sit up and take note. Every Thursday, checks would come in the mail for me, and he was beginning to change his perception. Today, four years later, he's completely involved in the business, and hopes to flee Corporate America too.

Network marketing is the perfect vehicle for people our age. Many of us Baby Boomers are successful, but we're looking at retirement and realizing it's not what we thought it was going to be. We want and can create more, while using all of the talents and skills we've developed over the years. Network marketing provides us with a proven system in which to do that. The best part is that we can spend time together helping others achieve their dreams, while we realize ours at the same time.

What I love most about this business is the people. I've never been around so many positive, kindhearted individuals. No one is scratching their way around to get success. The teamwork is just phenomenal.

I was surprised that some of our friends distanced themselves once we decided to do network marketing. I know they look down at us, despite the fact that we have a beautiful home and a successful life. But I don't let it affect me. Since network marketing, I've done a lot of work on personal growth, and so we naturally gravitate toward others who do the same.

Diane's Words of Wisdom

Finding success in this industry takes two skills: persistence and consistency. Get good at those and your life will never be the same.

Chapter Five

Get Real

> Nothing we can do can change the past, but everything we do changes the future.
>
> *Yogi Berra*

Okay, friends. Buckle up. It's time to get serious about our current situation. The housing market has crashed. Job security is obsolete. Social security is in the toilet, and we're almost better off investing in our mattresses than the stock market.

That's right, folks—the name of the game has changed. So we need to stop playing by the same old rules.

It's time to get our heads out of the sand. It's time to face some facts.

First, most people are broke. No matter how much money they make, it's gone at the end of the month. And with multiple credit cards, an upside-down home and some high-priced student loans, their debt is spiraling out of control. At the rate they're going, the only career that could possibly wipe it out is either illegal or involves some form of nudity. Meanwhile, financial advisors are telling us that our daily Starbucks habit is the cause of our money woes. *Give us a break.* Lattes are not the problem, people. Our *jobs* are.

Hey, you with the golden handcuffs. We're talking to you too!

You're dreadfully unhappy at work, and the rest of us are miserable just hearing about it. You sulk on Sunday nights like a toddler, and treat Fridays like you've been released from jail. You spend 80% of your week waiting for 20% of it to roll around, and when it does, you're so tired from all the prep work, commuting and errands that you have no energy to enjoy it. On top of that, you play endless tag-team with your babysitters and then wonder why your kids are so unglued.

You're trading time for money, marching to work every day like a rat in the race to make a buck. You have no back-up plan—nothing to sustain you in case of an emergency, disability, illness or family crisis. Every morning is Groundhog Day, with you dressed in a *different* version of the *same* suit, hoping this year you might get a better desk, office, title or paycheck. You never do. And when you're disappointed with your job, you run out to find another one *just like it*.

And you're making fun of *network marketing*?

We know, we know—everyone says, "You're so lucky just to be employed." *No, you're not!* Don't sell yourself short! You're not *lucky* to be working 60 hour weeks for 40-hour pay, or wondering from day to day whether you'll be employed this time next year. You are not *blessed* to wake up to an alarm clock and beg for unpaid leave. You weren't *spared* when you were demoted, downsized, furloughed and deprived of all your benefits, instead of losing your job.

When did *that* become good fortune?

Have you taken a look around lately? Your retirement fund has vanished. Social security is everything *but* secure, and at the rate our country is going, you won't be able to retire until you're dead. If you happen to make it before then, statistics suggest you'll be living on less than half the income you had before. So it might be time to lose those visions of climbing the Great Wall of China and boating down a Venice canal. *Not gonna happen.*

By the way, how is your health? Are you happy with the way you feel? Are you tired of getting six hours of sleep at night and hitting the snooze button with the force of a missile? Does it take three cups of coffee just to do your job? Are you comfy there, eating at your desk? Are you happy with the way you look, other than on paper?

Hey, we know that some of you love your jobs, and others of you are satisfied with the money you make. We're genuinely happy for you. But this is *not* about whether you like your career or your bank account. This is about whether you like your *life.*

It's time to launch a back-up plan before your boss does it for you. It's time to create some space and freedom to really enjoy your days. It's time to stop subscribing to the mob mentality that this is the best that you can do.

Trust us, it's not.

Hey, business owners! Have a seat. We need to chat.

So you did it—you finally gave your boss the finger and struck out on your own. *High five!* You're an artist, an author, an expert, an inventor, an *entrepreneur* (isn't that a neat word?). You're the rebel of your family and the envy of your friends. You relish your newfound freedom and boss-less life. You don't miss those office politics and stuffy corporate meetings. You have jeans to wear and lunches to write off! Never mind that you work 16-hour days and forget to shower. You love what you do! You could do it all day—hunkering down in your dungeon of creativity, with your dreams, charts, graphs and vision boards of just how you'll *hit it big*.

Good for *you*.

Or maybe you're not trying to win the start-up jackpot and instead you just want to be your own boss. Maybe you're a professional—a doctor, a lawyer, a dentist or accountant. No buy-outs or huge mergers in your future—just plain old freedom and your name on the door. Feels good, doesn't it?

We all agree that this world couldn't survive without the innovation, drive and imagination of people like you. It's the foundation of our country, the beauty of the human race and the basis for almost *all* progress. So, our hats off to you, business owners! We dig you.

But we definitely don't envy you.

Let's be honest. That tax write-off isn't so great when you have no income to protect. Family vacations are no fun when your laptop comes along. Going to sleep whenever you want is not so easy when the weight of the world comes with you. Sure, you don't miss a soccer game or recital; you're just on the Blackberry while you're there. You know it's true. Your stack of paperwork is taller than your kid. Your inbox is flooded with nonsense you have no time to read. And just how did so many government agencies find out where you live?

How 'bout those employees, huh? Who knew they could be this much work? They're so darn pushy with their ergonomic needs and payroll demands. Don't they know you have no time for employee handbooks and sexual harassment training? You have a business to run! There's real estate to lease, a website to build, insurance to buy, contracts to write, taxes to pay, logos to make, flyers to print, vendors to meet, clients to please, papers to file, *files* to file, licenses, registrations, and trash to take out (remember when you used to have a janitor?). Can't you get a *break*?

And just between you and us, are you lonely? We know how it is. You don't miss those annoying co-workers, but it would be fun to have a little water cooler chit-chat now and then, right? Let's face it, isolation is tough. But the idea of another networking function makes you want to gag.

Look, we hate to state the obvious—especially because we know how much you love the title of *Founder*—but unless you can walk away tomorrow and survive, it looks like all you *found* was another job.

Wouldn't it be nice to have some start-up money—a slush fund to help you launch a little quicker? Wouldn't it be great not to have to trade your first born for some venture capital, especially now that the banks won't give you a dime? Can you imagine how wonderful it would be to have enough money for real health insurance? Or *dental* insurance? Or *any* insurance?

We hear you, you don't want to give up your passion. Network marketing just doesn't compare to owning your own gig. It's not creative, industrious or bold. It's not... *original.*

We agree. It's just not the same. But in case you haven't noticed, we're trying to earn a living, not a Nobel Peace Prize. We want to stay at home with our kids as much as you do. We want to wear our flip-flops to meetings, too. We want money for our hobbies, our passions, our recreation and our futures... *just like you.*

So now that you know how great the opportunity is in network marketing, especially compared to the low risk, we have just one question. What kind of an entrepreneur would you be if you passed it up?

Wait! We're not done yet. Stay-at-home moms—drop that sippy cup and come over here for a sec...

You are the *true* heroes—the ones fighting the battle on the front lines. You take on the meanest of ear infections, the largest of laundry stacks, the loudest of temper tantrums, and the dirtiest of diapers, dishes, counters and fingers. You are everything to everyone—cook, maid, wife, mom, assistant, peacekeeper and CEO. True, it's the hardest job of your life, but you've got it all under control. And you wouldn't even *think* about going back to that corner office with those rock-star benefits, because *you* have the best title of all—*Mom.*

Sure, you're starved for some adult conversation, and even make unnecessary grocery store runs just to engage the clerk. Yeah, you'd give your right arm for eight consecutive hours of sleep. Oh, who are we kidding? *Six*. And so what if *Mickey Mouse Clubhouse* on replay is starting to feel like a form of medieval water torture? You wouldn't trade this for the world!

We get it. The luxury of being able to stay at home with your kids is one of life's greatest gifts. But let's get real, wouldn't you like to have some more dough? Just a little slush-fund so you could stop hearing so much about that nasty "B" word—*budget*? Admit it—you miss those designer jeans and mani-pedis, or that buttery leather tote you traded for that enormous diaper bag. That fuller than full-time job would look a heck of a lot better after a massage or two, right? It's ok, you can tell us.

Wouldn't it be nice to have a little creativity, fun and camaraderie back in your life? Or an excuse to get out of the house so you can hang with your friends? Wouldn't controlling the purse strings be a lot more fun when *your* money is in it?

Don't be afraid to fess up—you want a little "somethin'-somethin'" of your own. It's not selfish; it's *normal*.

We know network marketing won't give you that fancy job back or an expense account that doesn't quit; but if you dust off those talents of yours, it just *might* give you the perks that came with 'em.

So tell your man to take that budget and shove it, sister. Let's roll.

Baby Boomers! Grab your bifocals, this part is for you.

You've put in the work and you've done the time. Now bring on the next chapter of life, right? We know that you're ready for it; we can tell you've got plans. You have hobbies to learn, lessons to take, boats to sail and golf clubs to buy. And wouldn't that bedroom look nice as a gym?

Go for it. Who's going to stop you? Certainly not us. *You deserve it* – your nest is empty, your dues are paid. So break out those travel guides, and chill that champagne! Life has just begun!

Or so you thought.

Actually, this time isn't what you thought it would be, is it? The second you got an empty nest, you got an empty retirement fund too. What happened to all that money? Wasn't that investment supposed to be "low-risk?" How will you get that income back? Where do you go from here?

All of a sudden, the world is upside-down. Computer whiz kids are getting jobs that people with forty years of experience deserve. Employees with decades of loyalty under their belt are getting laid off. And just when you thought you were done taking care of other people, you find yourself juggling more needs than ever before. You've got aging parents to shuttle to doctors appointments, grown kids who need financial help, and grandkids you want to spend more time with. You're stuck in a generation sandwich, caught between your bills, *their* bills, walkers, car seats, and more.

So much for a life of leisure.

Well, in case you haven't caught on, we have a solution—one that allows you to re-secure your financial future *and* give you the freedom and flexibility to finally relax. Not only that, it gives you the chance to expand your circle, make new friends, get re-energized, and feel useful and valuable again.

With network marketing, the job description is simple: *Friendly company seeks enthusiastic individuals who love helping people and are willing to learn. Life experience a plus. Work wherever and whenever you want.*

So, what do you say? Think you fit the bill?

Listen, we realize that it's not fun to be scared of retirement, or to have to think about your money all over again. We know that in this day and age, you might not be able to get the job or the income you so clearly deserve. But cheer up, friends. With network marketing, you might be able to find something better... *and a lot more fun.*

Get the Facts

- According to a Harvard University study, only 45% of workers recently surveyed said they were happy at their jobs—the lowest in 22 years of polling. [xiv]

- Depression rates are ten times higher today than they were in 1960, and every year the age threshold of unhappiness sinks lower. [xv]

- The 40-hour workweek was originally designed to give Americans *more* time and *more* freedom. The Fair Labor Standards Act (29 U.S. Code Chapter 8), as first proposed under the New Deal, was one of the first pieces of legislation to reduce the workweek for certain industries to a maximum of 44 hours (down from 50, and before that, 60). [xvi]

- As of December 2010, Americans now owe more on their student loans than they do on their credit cards—a debt fast approaching $1 trillion, with no end in sight. America's student debt at the end of 2010 was nearly $880 billion. That number is growing by more than $2,800 per second. [xvii]

- In total, $50.8 billion worth of student loans were in default by the end of the 2009 fiscal year, compared with $39.1 billion at the end of the 2008 fiscal year. [xviii]

- According to the Department of Commerce, over 1 million people start traditional businesses each year. 40% of them fail within the first year. Of the remaining businesses, 80% fail within the next five years. Of those, another 80% fail within the subsequent five years. [xix]

- According to the Wall Street Journal, banks—under scrutiny by regulators—are continuing to strengthen capital reserves, making it difficult even for entrepreneurs with track records and years of experience to qualify for business loans. [xx]

- In 2009, American venture-capital funds raised just $9.1 billion in the second quarter, down from $33 billion during the peak year of 2000. [xxi]

Chapter Six

Get a Plan

It's time to get real about your money, honey.

So far, you've figured out that it doesn't grow on trees. That's good. But have you noticed lately that it also doesn't grow in the stock market or in bank accounts?

Unfortunately, your house is no breadwinner either. It went from being an asset to a liability overnight, or as renowned financial expert, Robert Kiyosaki, calls it, "a credit card with shingles and a driveway."

If you think your job is an investment, think again. The average wages for the middle class haven't gone up in 10 years. And unless you consider a gold watch and pat on the back to be a good return on a 35-year investment, it's a loser. Besides, when you switch companies, you're back at square one.

Now let's talk about your savings account. First, congrats on even having one! In this economy, you are a rare breed. But what will it be worth a few years from now, when inflation skyrockets, but your balance doesn't? What can a savings account really do for you anyway, aside from offer a few bucks in the case of an emergency or retail splurge? And what will you do after it gets wiped out?

Seriously, what happens when you don't want to work anymore? Or worse, *can't* work anymore? What if you or your spouse gets laid off? What will you do when a family member needs your help? Or you want another baby, a new car, home, wedding, or college fund? What are your options for creating additional or passive income?

As you can see from the diagram on the following page, you don't really have many.

First, whether it's a CD, Money Market Account or savings account, you have to *have* money to make money. At the current interest rates, to make an extra $200 a month in passive income, you'd have to have more than $120,000 sitting in the bank as we speak. That's right, *sitting*.

To earn $200 per month		To earn $600 per month	
Interest Rate	Amount in the Bank	Interest Rate	Amount in the Bank
2%	$120,000.00	2%	$362,000.00
3%	$80,000.00	3%	$240,000.00
4%	$60,000.00	4%	$180,000.00
5%	$48,000.00	5%	$144,000.00
6%	$40,000.00	6%	$120,000.00
7%	$34,286.00	7%	$102,857.00
8%	$30,000.00	8%	$90,000.00
9%	$26,666.80	9%	$80,001.00
10%	$24,000.00	10%	$72,000.00

To earn $800 per month		To earn $1,000 per month	
Interest Rate	Amount in the Bank	Interest Rate	Amount in the Bank
2%	$480,000.00	2%	$600,000.00
3%	$320,000.00	3%	$400,000.00
4%	$240,000.00	4%	$300,000.00
5%	$192,000.00	5%	$240,000.00
6%	$160,000.00	6%	$200,000.00
7%	$137,143.00	7%	$171,429.00
8%	$120,000.00	8%	$150,000.00
9%	$106,667.00	9%	$133,334.80
10%	$96,000.00	10%	$120,000.00

To earn $5,000 per month		To earn $10,000 per month	
Interest Rate	Amount in the Bank	Interest Rate	Amount in the Bank
2%	$3,000,000.00	2%	$6,000,000.00
3%	$2,000,000.00	3%	$4,000,000.00
4%	$1,500,000.00	4%	$3,000,000.00
5%	$1,200,000.00	5%	$2,400,000.00
6%	$1,000,000.00	6%	$2,000,000.00
7%	$857,143.00	7%	$1,714,285.00
8%	$750,000.00	8%	$1,500,000.00
9%	$666,668.00	9%	$1,333,335.00
10%	$600,000.00	10%	$1,200,000.00

This chart reflects how residual income is created from a traditional savings account.

Even if the interest rates improve to 5% in the near future, you'd still have to have $48,000 *available* to invest— all to receive that same $200 a month.

Most of us don't have that kind of money sitting around. And even if we did, it wouldn't be worth it to plop it in some account that moves like a snail. You'd have to get started at the age of 20 for it to be worth it by the time you're 65.

So what's the answer? Something with a little more risk and a lot more reward? The stock market, maybe?

That *might* have been the answer in 1985, but as a lot of broke Baby Boomers will tell you today, ten years ago they would have been better off putting their money into high stakes poker than the NASDAQ. Since the Great Depression, the stock market has crashed three times. *Two* of those times were in the last ten years.

Now do you think network marketing looks silly?

Listen, we think it's great that some of you have no debt, and that you've managed to put a few pennies away for a rainy day. But you shouldn't have any illusions about just how far that will get you—in this economy or *at all*.

Nowhere else is there a lower investment with a higher rate of return than in network marketing. For less than a few hundred bucks, you get the chance to earn $200 a month, $1000 a month, $10,000 a month and more, in far less time. And unlike almost every other opportunity around, you don't have to put yourself into debt first, spending twenty years of your life paying back your loans one cent at a time—all *before* you have enough to invest.

Are you catching on?

Day in and out, we hear from smug friends who inquire about how our network marketing businesses are doing after ten or twelve weeks. *Puh-lease*. What were your stocks making after 90 days in the market? How much interest was in your savings account after the first few months? Were you rolling in the dough after three months at your entry-level job?

Wake up, folks. It's time to take a critical look at why certain things in our society are respected, and others are rejected.

Yes, we know that in network marketing there's *no* guarantee. But unlike a lot of other options covered here, the outcome is largely within your control. So before you go throwing your money at the next broker or banker you see, consider putting it into the wisest investment of all—*you*.

Get the Facts

- According to an article in Business Week, as Baby Boomers age, there will be more retirees collecting benefits and fewer workers paying taxes. The current Social Security program is fiscally sound until 2041, at which time it will cover 80% of promised benefits. But with privatization, the Social Security budget shortfall would arrive as early as 2017. [xxii]

- When Social Security was adopted in The United States in 1935, the retirement age was set at 65, but life expectancy was 62.5 years old. The average person died before they could collect. [xxiii]

- As of July 2010, both Republican and Democratic leaders of the House of Representatives indicated that the retirement age will likely be raised to 70 over the next few years, a change that will impact the Social Security benefits of all people ages 50 and younger. [xxiv]

- According to the AARP, many Baby Boomers cannot afford to retire because of the recession, sharp decline in housing prices, rapidly rising prices for food, gasoline and utilities, and stock market losses, which have cut into the value of 401(k) savings. [xxv]

Chapter Seven

Get Involved

> A woman is the full circle. Within her is
> the power to create, nurture and transform.
>
> *Diane Mariechild*

It's a level playing field, ladies. So get in the game.

That's right. Network marketing is one of the only places where women have *none* of the limitations of mainstream society. No barriers, boys clubs, glass ceilings, or salary gaps. No full-time hours, hellish commutes or skimpy maternity leave. It's one of the most equitable compensation options around.

But that's not the only reason why women outnumber men in this business 4 to 1. Here are a few more.

It's Second Nature

Like we said, the opportunity in network marketing is equal on paper, but in reality we women actually have a gigantic genetic edge. It's a business where many of our greatest strengths—socializing, connecting, nurturing, teaching, and relating—are *part of the job*. It's a place where sharing, talking, togetherness, camaraderie and teamwork enhance the bottom line.

Now *that's* what we call a learning curve.

Don't get us wrong. It's not like we sit around all day singing songs and braiding each other's hair. Network marketing can really be hard work at times—facing rejection, battling the stigma, and working with diverse personality types. But it is a place where we can be who we are, and instantly be good at what we do. Imagine that. You haven't even started and already you're a natural!

Women are also attracted to the sense of community that comes from network marketing. Men may tease us about the fact that we go to the ladies room together, but it's true—we like to travel in packs. Network marketing gives us the chance to do that, but in a financially productive way. In this business, individual success equals group success, and competition is to our *dis*advantage. Sure we might be stereotyped as catty by some, but we know the truth. Women want to triumph *together*. Now, we can.

Women Need This Now More Than Ever

It's the 21st Century. We fought, we picketed, we protested, we won. Now here we are, standing on the shoulders of our female ancestors, and you know what? The view's not so great.

Sure, we can conquer Corporate America *and* still rule the roost. We can bring home the bacon *and* fry it up! We have choices! *Tons and tons of choices...*

But for some reason we're still stuck. We know we can *have* it all. We're just not sure how to *manage* it all.

Many of us are putting off having kids, because we're afraid that having a baby means losing a career. Then we're faced with the hazard of bearing children later in life. Or planning it in the sweet spot—where neither professional success, nor biological clock, is a threat. Some of us are delaying marriage, figuring that our chances for career growth, travel and independence might be compromised if we don't. Then we end up dealing with the pitfalls of being single, and alone, in a dual income world.

Others of us are settling down, building homes and having families, only to realize that we worked all those years to get so educated, so qualified, so experienced... for what? And still some of us are doing it all—holding down the fort *and* the job—maybe because we want to, or maybe because we have to. Either way, we can barely breathe.

We're not saying that network marketing is the only way to have your cake and eat it too. We're just saying that as far as balancing, juggling, managing and *savoring* each slice, it's about the best option we've ever seen.

> Building a network marketing business is uniquely compatible with the demands of raising a family.
>
> Kim Kiyosaki, Author

Women Want to Make a Difference

We love our independence, but what we really want is *influence*.

For women, the ability to effect change and make an impact is paramount. We don't just want to better ourselves. We want to better our children, our schools, our communities and our planet.

According to the U.S. Bureau of Labor Statistics, only 1 in 4 Americans engaged in volunteer work between late 2007 and 2008. And women outnumbered men in that regard by almost 30%. On top of that, women across nearly every income level give significantly more to charity than men, nearly twice as much in some cases.

So what's the answer to saving the world? That's easy—give women more time and money!

That sounds great on paper, but the reality is that we're not likely to have either anytime soon. Without a Sugar Daddy or some unexpected windfall, most women are not in the position to move out of financial stability and into dramatic wealth. Just fifteen Fortune 500 companies are run by women, and according to *Forbes Magazine*, women represent only 2% of the world's self-made billionaires. Sure, we're gaining on our male counterparts when it comes to equal opportunities, but we're still limited as far as our ability to *take advantage* of them.

For most of us, basic survival is a day-to-day chore. Our schedule is consumed with getting money in the door, food on the table and our kids shuttled to and from play dates, activities and doctors appointments. Any extra time we have is spent engaging in pure luxury, also known as shuttling *ourselves* to the rare play date, activity or doctor appointment. And until we can do more than just keep our heads above water, our chances of having enough time or money for global influence are limited.

Network marketing changes those odds. By offering women a shot at creating substantial passive income just by doing what comes naturally, network marketing provides the time and money for us to give back to society *and* leave our mark.

Look, we're not saying that women can't save the world one *hour* or *dollar* at a time. We're just saying that it would be easier with a lot more of both.

Speaking of making a difference, wouldn't it be nice to make a *permanent* difference in the life of someone you love? Well, now you can. Network marketing gives you the ability to empower your friends and family with the tools to improve their situation *themselves*. We're not talking about a handout; we're talking about a hand *up*.

Everybody has strengths. Everyone has talents, knowledge and a unique skill-set all their own. Some people love socializing and are naturals at public speaking, teaching and training, while others have a talent for writing, are great at following up, and are masters at managing the details. Whatever the case, network marketing gives you the chance to reach out to someone in your life—someone who might not have the specific strengths they need to achieve their goals alone—and say, "Hey, let's do this together."

So, now you can do more than just *listen* to your friends' problems; you can help *solve* them. *That's* a big difference to make.

Okay, we can't get out of this chapter without talking about wealth and your relationship to it. Not to get all "self-help-y" on you, but what's your relationship with abundance? Do you believe that you are allowed to have an abundance of time, freedom and money?

Are you resistant to having *riches*? Does the word "*riches*" turn you off? Do you think that fancy cars, jets and luxury travel are for the boys? If you see a woman enjoying these things, do you assume she married into them?

Most women have an image in their mind of the independently wealthy woman—she's greedy, pushy, selfish and masculine. She wears power suits and plays poker with the guys. And above all, she's heartless.

But is that true?

What if we told you that the wealthy women we know are fun, fearless, kind, compassionate, philanthropic, free and *feminine*? Does that change your impression of money? Does it alter your perception of *your* right to own it?

Making money and having abundance is your natural born right. So when did you associate it with men? Or negativity and greed? How old were you when you were told that money was dirty? Or that you should feel guilty for wanting it? When did you decide that being poor was honorable?

Well, it's time for some reprogramming.

Having money is not about being materialistic or judging others for what they don't have. And it's not the most important thing in life. But you know what? It can pay for what is. Whether that's a roof over your head, health insurance, medical bills, your child's college education, a way to quit your job, the ability to fund an orphanage in

Africa or provide clean water for the world, the freedom to choose is yours. And money pays for that freedom.

We don't want you to be impressed with the living we've earned; we want you to feel empowered by it. Empowered to stop settling for less and start expecting more. Empowered to get over your money baggage and silence that inner guilt. Empowered to get out there and *claim your piece of the pie.* It's yours. Go get it. And then... *share* it.

Besides, whoever said that money can't buy happiness is obviously still cleaning her own house.

Get the Facts

- In 2009, women earned 77 cents for every $1 earned by men. [xxvi]

- As of 2006, women are expected to live an average of five to seven years longer than men. [xxvii]

- As of 2008, of the elderly living in poverty, three out of four are women. [xxviii]

- Single women are some of the poorest in the world. Over 84% of single-parent households in the United States are headed by mothers. Most of them are not in the work force. [xxix]

- According to a 2009 Census Bureau report, in 2008, 29.9% of female householders with no husband were below the poverty level. [xxx]

- On average, women spend 17 years of their lives caring for children and 18 years assisting aged parents. [xxxi]

Chapter Eight

Get Over It

> If you're ever going to doubt something, doubt your limits.
>
> *Don Ward*

We'll be the first to admit it: not everyone is a fit for network marketing. For example, if you're married to your title, your corner office or your image, *don't* do network marketing. If your favorite part of the high school reunion is handing out your business cards, *don't* do network marketing. If you regularly make public service announcements about how important your job is, *don't* do network marketing. If you love a corporation or entity that doesn't love you back, *don't* do network marketing. If you need instant gratification, are paralyzed by rejection or require the approval of people you've never met, *don't* do network marketing. If you've gotten through this book and are still skeptical of network marketing, it obviously isn't for you. So, please, *don't* do network marketing.

Seriously though, just because network marketing carries the promise of a gigantic payoff doesn't mean it's without its own trials or tribulations. You'd be hard-pressed to find one success story that doesn't come with its own distinct rocky road.

But that's not just the price of network marketing; that's the price of *life*. Either you're in the game or you're not. And if you're in it, there's a chance you'll get bumped, bruised, pushed and shoved. If you can't take it, go back to the bleachers.

It's completely cliché, but if you want something you've never had, you must do something you've never done. That means move outside your comfort zone.

We know. You like your comfort zone. It's *comfortable*. But you know what else is comfortable? Your recliner. And a bowl of Mac 'n' Cheese. But that doesn't mean either is good for your "bottom line." If you want real comfort—*lifelong* comfort—you have to be prepared for a little discomfort and personal growth in the present moment. Whether it's starting a new diet, workout program, or heading off to get a four-year degree, the rules are the same: delayed gratification is just that—*delayed*. Get used to it.

And so what if network marketing comes with a little rejection? You've never been rejected before? You've never been turned down for a job or a date? You got accepted to every school to which you applied? Okay then. Get over it, and move on.

Speaking of moving on, it might be time to move along from something else too—the unsupportive and negative friends in your life. That's right. Unfortunately, some of the people closest to you might actually be the problem. We know you care what they think. That's okay. But did you choose them wisely? Are they supportive of your ultimate purpose in life? Or are they threatened by your success, afraid that if you reach out and pursue something better, they might have to, too?

Take it from us, when you make the decision to take control of your future—to break free from the norm and challenge the status quo—all bets are off. You never know what your friends and family will do. Some will support you, others will join you. Some will reject you, others will ignore you. Some will ridicule you to your face, others behind your back. Whatever the case, it has everything to do with them, and nothing to do with you.

The real question is not whether your friends are impressed with you, but whether YOU are impressed with you. Did you accomplish everything you set out to? Are you achieving everything you are capable of? Are you living the life of your dreams? Well if you're not, then you're most likely working for someone who is.

Besides, who cares if your friends think you're a fool for trying network marketing? We think they're fools for *not* trying network marketing. And why would you take advice from someone who isn't living the life you want anyway?

Don't bother with people who criticize your effort to secure a better life for you and your family. That's not what friends do. Remember, misery loves company. And misery will do anything to get it, including disguising itself as care and concern. So don't buy into it. Don't take the bait. Your loved ones, while trying to be protective, can be some of the most disabling forces around. As we said in the Introduction, we know this firsthand.

In the end, only you can decide how committed you are to living the life you want. If you're willing to get the true reward of ultimate happiness—whether through network marketing or any other endeavor—the price of admission is always the same: your ego. For you to get in, it has to stay out.

> Don't unknowingly appoint your friends as designated drivers of your life. If you don't worry about your future, no one else will. Your friends will struggle far more with your financial success than they will with your hardships.
>
> Dr. Tom Barrett, Author and Network Marketing Expert

Take our word for it—it's impossible to flip your mindset around people who have the exact same mindset *you used to have*. So if you want evidence that network marketing will work for you, align yourself with the people who've made it work for them, not the ones who haven't. Or worse, the ones who haven't even tried.

And while we're at it, unless you love it, don't stick with your current job just because you're good at it. Or because it's what you do, who you are, or what you went to school for. Don't underestimate yourself. You're good at a lot of things. Those things are waiting for you.

So there you have it. If you're not willing to get over yourself, get a dream, get going and get a great life, then we have just one last request. *Please*, get out of the way.

Conclusion

We didn't write this book *just* to get in your face about your life, or to pick on your friends and your job. We promise. We wrote it because we care, and because we want you to know what we know, so that you can have what so many of us in this industry have—a truly prosperous and joyful life.

Too many people are censoring their hopes and dreams these days, silencing that inner voice inside of them demanding to know *"Is this all there is?"* It's not. We know it's not. But don't take our word for it. Find out for yourself.

It's time to get your feet off the ground, and put your head in the clouds. It's time to dust off that pipe dream and take it out for a spin. It's time to evaluate the menu of options in front of you and feel empowered to say "No thanks. I'd like to order something different, something *better.*" You deserve it. *All of it.* And you deserve it now, not *someday.*

We can't promise that network marketing will make you rich, or that it will be a breeze. We can't promise that people won't ridicule your decision to do it, or tell you to "Dream on." But we can promise you that if you lock arms with us, and the millions of people all around the world just like us, it will be well worth the ride.

Don't wonder what will happen if you fail. Wonder what will happen if you succeed. Trust us, there's far more around the bend than you ever imagined is possible. Consider this book your fork in the road. It's up to you to take the turn.

Afterword

This book isn't about *our stories*. It's really about your story, including the parts you've yet to write. But we decided to include a few more details about our individual journeys in this Afterword, so that you get a better idea of where our passion comes from, in case you catch a glimpse of yourself.

Lory (Daughter), Flip-Flop CEO
BA, Interdisciplinary Studies: Marketing
Communications and Spanish
Network Marketer

When I first found out about network marketing, I was shocked. I had no idea that anything like this existed. I was searching for freedom from what everyone else considered to be "the real world." Although I was successful in it, I had zero passion for Corporate America. Work was time-consuming and I was miserable. Being fresh out of college and young, I missed my spring breaks, my flip-flops and waking up without an alarm clock. My dream life was quickly becoming my biggest nightmare. I wanted out.

I began to search for something better. I kept my eyes wide open for other possibilities. I was not opposed to trying something new or different or "outside" the box. In fact, I welcomed it. As long as it took me far away from this lifestyle that I was beginning to resent. Being naïve was such a blessing because, looking back, I didn't have any preconceived ideas about this industry. I thought it was brilliant, so I jumped in with both feet.

I quickly discovered the stigma that surrounded network marketing, beginning at home. The one person I wanted to pursue this with was my mom, but she wanted nothing to do with it. I couldn't understand how her aversion for an industry could be so strong, when it made so much sense to me. As it turned out, a lot of my friends felt the same way she did. They thought I was crazy. But I thought *they* were crazy. We were gridlocked. And for a while, nothing changed. It was a trying time.

Then, after a year of not seeing *any* results, my determination to keep going finally paid off. Thank goodness quitting was *never* an option. When my mom and I finally joined forces, we were unstoppable.

We didn't let other people determine our future. We knew what was possible in this business and in life, and we were confident that we could create that for ourselves. Together we were better. Her strengths were my weaknesses, her weaknesses were my strengths. As a team, we were able to reach the top of the company within a year.

No one can tell us that network marketing doesn't work, when we are living proof that it does. I believe this is possible for anyone who wants it. I realize that not everyone wants it. But anyone who does want more choices in their life can have them. They just have to be willing to *go for it.*

I don't believe there is a right or wrong way to live, but I definitely believe it's a choice. We all have choices. Network marketing is not an "either-or;" it's choosing both—time *and* money, making a difference *and* making a living, being a mom *and* a provider.

I love that when I wake up every day, I get to choose how to spend it. How I spend my days is how I spend my life, so having the freedom to live my life on my terms means raising my kids while raising the abundance in this world.

Lory's Words of Wisdom

If you love what you do, keep doing it!! This isn't about quitting your job in order to "do" network marketing. This is about incorporating it into your life and having more choices. Then you can decide what you want to do. Listen to your heart above all other voices, and never ever give up!

Janine (Mother), Flip-Flop CEO
Associate of Arts Degree
Network Marketer

When Lory told me how excited she was about this "new" career that she'd discovered, I thought she was crazy. She had *no* idea what she was getting herself into. As someone who'd been approached years before, in a very secretive and misleading way, I wanted Lory to understand what she was getting into. I believed that the business had *nothing* to do with marketing and *everything* to do with using your relationships with family and friends for personal gain. I wanted no part of it, and I could not see myself, or my daughter, as "one of those people!"

After a year of us battling over our respective truths, I decided to look for a way to show her just how naïve she was being, and how absurd it would be to give up the amazing career she'd worked so hard to have. So I began to do my own due diligence. As I did, the opposite outcome occurred. I found out just how much things had transformed over the prior thirty years… changes that took this industry from being an embarrassment to being one of the best opportunities around. I finally "got" it, and realized how bigoted I had been. It was as if my life had suddenly flipped right side up… for the very first time.

As they say, what goes around comes around. So the second I shifted my paradigm, I was faced with skepticism and hurtful judgments by the people in *my* life. It was a challenging time. Some days it still is. But I know that I could never go back to working for someone else's dream again. All those years that I struggled as a single mom, and couldn't be there for my girls because I was working, I get to do differently today, with my grandchildren. Now that I've discovered a business that I can work around my priorities, I never feel like I'm *working*.

As a stay at home grandma, I get to be at every "mom's group" activity, enjoy long lunches with my girlfriends, and take trips with my daughters whenever we want to. I never have to choose between being there for my family and having a thriving career. It's a freedom and lifestyle that I cannot help but want to share with others. Network marketing is a way to not only make a great income, but to make a difference as well. Our business gives us the opportunity to work on ourselves, to become the best person that we can be, and to help others do the same. It's a business founded on empowering others to attain their dreams, with a financial structure attached that rewards you in direct proportion to your accomplishments.

Never has there been a more crucial time to bring clarity and understanding to a model whose time has come. This business is the *best kept secret* around, and now that I've seen the light at the end of the tunnel, I want to be that light for others. We believe it's time to provide some updated information about this industry! We hope our book can provide that.

Janine's Words of Wisdom

If you're not a dreamer naturally, learn to be one. The most valuable thing I've learned these past seven years is the importance of knowing what you want. You don't have to know *how* you'll get there, but you get exactly what you think about. So, think about what you want, instead of what you don't want! When your why is big enough, and clear enough, the *how* will take care of itself!

Whitney (Writer), Flip-Flop CEO

BA, Political Science and Sociology
Juris Doctor
Network Marketer

When I met Lory and Janine, I was a recovering attorney, semi-retired entrepreneur and freelance writer, taking the occasional gig to bankroll my lazy life at the beach. I thought I'd done it all. I'd rejected Corporate America when I left the practice of law at age 27; I'd followed my dreams of self-employment when I started a business that ultimately led to greater freedom; and I'd created passive income by self-publishing a textbook that had unexpected success. In my mind, I was everything but a network marketer.

On top of that, I tried to avoid them at all costs.

As a business owner, I'd been a member of many different networking organizations, and was exhausted from colliding with pushy people who swore that I would get rich quick if I'd just give them five minutes of my time. I never met one person who was rich, let alone quick, and I found the whole thing to be ridiculous.

So when a friend asked me to consider writing a book with Lory and Janine about network marketing, I figured she'd lost her mind. I was *obviously* the wrong person for the job. I mean, it's one thing to hire someone full of sass; it's another to hire someone full of disdain. Besides, I was sure they couldn't afford my fee (I know, so rude).

Nonetheless, I agreed to the meeting because they seemed nice, and sincere in their mission to shed light on this industry. Plus, I got the part about the money wrong.

The rest, as they say, is history. After diving into the research on network marketing, my mind wasn't just opened, it was *changed*. I finally "got" the professional side of network marketing, which was so different from the style I'd been exposed to before. On top of that, I couldn't believe how many savvy, sophisticated, and fun people were already doing it with astounding success. Here I was, running to the ends of the Earth looking for financial freedom, and the best option was staring me in the face. Talk about being wrong.

So, without any encouragement from Lory and Janine, I jumped into network marketing while working on the book. When they saw that my belief in the industry had grown as strong as theirs, they invited me to put my name on it, too.

Eight months later, I'm already turning a sizable profit in my network marketing business. It hasn't always been a breeze, but it's a heck of a lot easier than all the other things I've done.

Like a lot of entrepreneurs, I want a big fat life. I want adventure, I want fun. I want to sample every delicious opportunity that comes my way. Network marketing is the vehicle that makes all of that possible now. I can't believe I almost missed it (ten times).

Today, I no longer think about what I want to do for a living. I think about what I want to do with my life.

Whitney's Words of Wisdom

You're only in this game once. Don't settle for being a spectator.

These are some of the books, CDs, websites and people that we love (we think you'll love them too). Additional resources can be found on our website at www.theflipflopceo.com.

Dare to Dream, Work to Win, Understanding the Dollars and Sense of Success in Network Marketing, Dr. Tom Barrett

The New Professionals, The Rise of Network Marketing as the Next Major Profession, James A. Robinson and Charles W. King

The Business of the 21st Century, Robert T. Kiyosaki, with John Fleming and Kim Kiyosaki, 2010

The Business School for People who Like Helping People, Robert T. Kiyosaki and Sharon L. Lechter, 2005

Brilliant Compensation Audio CD, Tim Sales

The 45-Second Business Presentation that Will Change Your Life, Don Failla,

www.FaillaPublications.com

The Slight Edge, Secret to a Successful Life, Jeff Olson

The Seven Habits of Highly Successful Network Marketing Professionals, Audio CD, Stephen R. Covey

Think and Grow Rich, Napoleon Hill

The Master Key to Riches, Napoleon Hill

The Success Formula, Bob Burg

Networking Times, www.networkingtimes.com

Dave Ramsey, www.daveramsey.com

ⁱ   Direct Selling Association, www.dsa.org

ⁱⁱ   Direct Selling Association, www.dsa.org

ⁱⁱⁱ World Federation of Direct Selling, www.wfdsa.org

ⁱᵛ   CNN Money, "Holiday shoppers head online this year," http://money.cnn.com/2010/11/29/technology/cyber_monday/index.htm, *Accessed March 5, 2011*

ᵛ   http://www.pcworld.com/businesscenter/article/221055/forrester_bullish_on_us_ecommerce_market.html, *Accessed March 5, 2011*

ᵛⁱ   Kiplinger, "More Workers Live Paycheck to Paycheck, CareerBuilder Finds," http://kiplinger.com/news/article.php/more-workers-live-paycheck-to-paycheck-19937927.html, *Accessed March 5, 2011*

ᵛⁱⁱ Take Control of Your Money, Dave Ramsey Live, Workbook, 2-4

ᵛⁱⁱⁱ Reuters, "US Consumer Bankruptcies Hit 5-Year High in 2010," http://www.reuters.com/article/2011/01/03/ba-bankruptcy-filings-idUSN0325868420110103, *Accessed March 5, 2011*

ⁱˣ   Take Control of Your Money, Dave Ramsey Live, Workbook, 2-4

ˣ   MSN, "Now, even lawyers are getting axed," http://www.msnbc.msn.com/id/30196250/ns/business-consumer_news/, *Accessed March 5, 2011*

ˣⁱ   The New York Times, "Job Losses in City Reach Up Ladder," www.nytimes.com/2008/12/12/nyregion/12jobs.html, *Accessed March 5, 2011*

ˣⁱⁱ The Hackett Group, "Acceleration of Offshoring Trend Driving Loss of Millions of Finance and IT Jobs in U.S. and Europe," http://www.thehackettgroup.com/about/alerts/alerts_2010/alert_12022010.jsp, *Accessed March 5, 2011*

ˣⁱⁱⁱ The Wall Street Journal Digital Network, "Employers Hit Salaried Staff With Furloughs," http://online.wsj.com/article/SB123542559566852689.html, *Accessed March 5, 2011*

xiv   Shawn Achor, The Happiness Advantage, As referenced in AOL Health, "Happiness at Work," http://www.aolhealth.com/2010/10/20/happiness-at-work/, *Accessed March 5, 2011*

xv   Shawn Achor, The Happiness Advantage, As referenced in AOL Health, "Happiness at Work," http://www.aolhealth.com/2010/10/20/happiness-at-work/, *Accessed March 5, 2011*

xvi   GoBankingRates.com, "Where the 40-Hour Workweek Came From and How it Hurt the Economy," http://www.gobankingrates.com/history-of-the-40-hour-work-week-and-its-effects-on-the-economy/, *Accessed March 5, 2011*

xvii   MSNBC, "Student Loans Leave Crushing Debt Burden," http://www.msnbc.msn.com/id/40772705/ns/business-cnbc_tv, *Accessed March 5, 2011*

xviii   The New York Times, "Student Loan Default Rates Come Under Scrutiny," http://thechoice.blogs.nytimes.com/2010/07/14/student-loan-default-rates-come-under-scrutiny, *Accessed March 5, 2011*

xix   Michael Gerber, The E-Myth Revisited, 2

xx   The Wall Street Journal, Start-Ups Will Keep Struggling in 2010," http://online.wsj.com/article/SB10001424052748703580904574638282624707184.html, *Accessed March 5, 2011*

xxi   The Wall Street Journal, Start-Ups Will Keep Struggling in 2010," http://online.wsj.com/article/SB10001424052748703580904574638282624707184.html, *Accessed March 5, 2011*

xxii   Bloomberg Business Week, "Social Security is Solid: Despite talk of a need for privatization, the U.S. government program still does the job and requires only modest tweaks: Pro or Con?" www.businessweek.com/debateroom/archives/2007/12/social_security_is_solid.html, *Accessed March 5, 2011*

xxiii   Maddy Dychtwald, Influence, 150-151

xxiv The Washington Times, "Both parties mull raising the retirement age," http://www.washingtontimes.com/news/2010/jul/13/both-parties-mull-raising-retirement-age/, *Accessed March 5, 2011*

xxv AARP Financial, "Why Boomers Can't Retire," http://www.aarpfinancial. com/content/Learning/retPerspectives_hinden_0708.cfm, *Accessed March 5, 2011*

xxvi Yahoo News, "U.S. Census Bureau Facts for Features: Women's History Month: March 2011, http://news.yahoo.com/s/usnw/20110222/pl_usnw/ DC52342, *Accessed March 5, 2011*

xxvii National Vital Statistics Report, June 28, 2010, Volume 58, Number 21

xxviii Center for American Progress, "Unmarried Women Hit Hard by Poverty," http://www.americanprogress.org/issues/2009/09/census_women.html, *Accessed March 5, 2011*

xxix U.S. Census Bureau, Current Population Reports, Consumer Income, Income, Poverty, and Health Insurance Coverage in the United States: 2008, September 2009 Issue, also available at http://www.census.gov/prod/2009pubs/ p60-236.pdf, *Accessed March 5, 2011*

xxx U.S. Census Bureau, Current Population Reports, Consumer Income, Income, Poverty, and Health Insurance Coverage in the United States: 2008, September 2009 Issue, also available at http://www.census.gov/prod/2009pubs/ p60-236.pdf, *Accessed March 5, 2011*

xxxi Maddy Dychtwald, Influence, 147, As referenced in The New York Times, "Mothers Bearing a Second Burden," May 14, 1989

All truth passes through three stages.
First, it is ridiculed.
Second, it is violently opposed.
Third, it is accepted as being self-evident.

Arthur Schopenhauer